UNIT B

The Changing Earth

Theme: Models

Y0-CAX-471

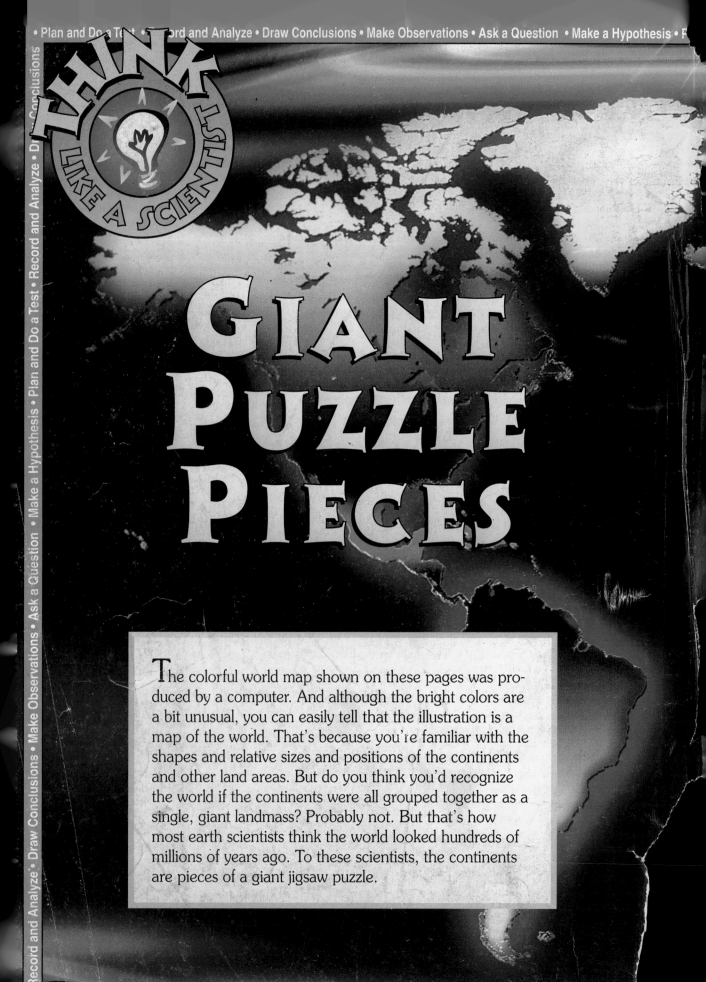

THINK LIKE A SCIENTIST

GIANT PUZZLE PIECES

The colorful world map shown on these pages was produced by a computer. And although the bright colors are a bit unusual, you can easily tell that the illustration is a map of the world. That's because you're familiar with the shapes and relative sizes and positions of the continents and other land areas. But do you think you'd recognize the world if the continents were all grouped together as a single, giant landmass? Probably not. But that's how most earth scientists think the world looked hundreds of millions of years ago. To these scientists, the continents are pieces of a giant jigsaw puzzle.

Coming Up

Computers are a vital tool in Anna M-M Hamann's work as a cartographer.

INVESTIGATION ①

DO CONTINENTS REALLY DRIFT ABOUT?

About 80 years ago, Alfred Wegener suggested that at one time all the continents were joined together in one large "supercontinent." Further, he suggested that the continents split apart and drifted to their current locations. Other scientists laughed at him. Could he have been right?

Activity

The Great Puzzle

Take a look at a map of the world. Notice that the continents seem to fit together like the pieces of a jigsaw puzzle. Can you reconstruct Wegener's supercontinent from today's continents?

MATERIALS
- scissors
- outline map of the continents
- sheet of paper
- glue
- map of the world
- *Science Notebook*

SAFETY ///////
Handle scissors with care.

Procedure

1. Your teacher will give you an outline map of Earth's continents. Using scissors, cut out each of the continents along the dark outlines.

2. Arrange the continents on a sheet of paper so that they all fit together, forming one supercontinent.

3. After you have obtained your best fit, make a map by gluing the pieces onto the sheet of paper in the pattern that you obtained. Keep your map in your Science Notebook.

4. Using a map of the world, locate the name of each continent for your map. Label the continents.

Step 1

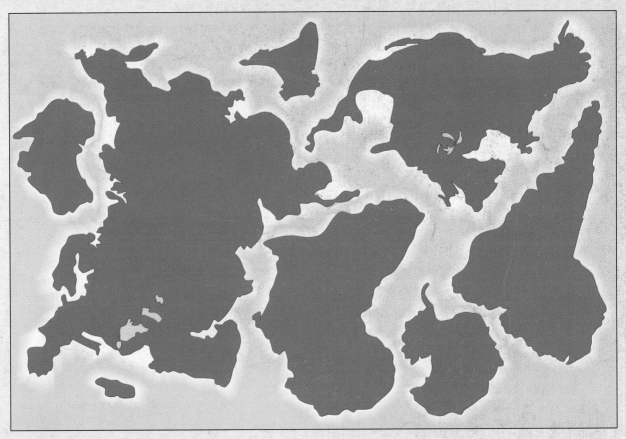

▲ Outline map of the continents

Analyze and Conclude

1. How well did the continents fit together to make a single supercontinent?

2. Compare the map that you made with one showing the present locations of the continents. What can you infer about Earth's continents if both maps are accurate?

3. In your reconstruction, what continents border the continent of North America?

4. What evidence, besides the shapes of the continents, might scientists look for to confirm Alfred Wegener's idea that continents were once joined in a supercontinent?

INVESTIGATE FURTHER!

RESEARCH

Look in a world atlas, such as *Goode's World Atlas*, to find a map that shows Earth's landforms. Use this information to explain why Wegener thought Earth's landmasses were once joined as a supercontinent.

Alfred Wegener and the Drifting Continents

Reading Focus What was Wegener's hypothesis about the movement of the continents?

The year was 1911. Nabisco introduced the Oreo cookie. Marie Curie won a Nobel Prize for isolating pure radium. The National Urban League was founded.

That same year, Alfred L. Wegener read a scientific paper that changed his life. The paper presented evidence that millions of years ago a land bridge may have connected South America with Africa. To Wegener the evidence suggested that the two continents were once a continuous landmass. From this he hypothesized that *all* of Earth's continents might once have been joined.

In 1912, Wegener gave a talk about his ideas on moving continents. He suggested that Earth's landmasses had once been joined and had since drifted apart. Most people in the scientific community thought Wegener's idea was ridiculous. Wegener still held on to his hypothesis.

In 1915, Wegener published a book explaining how Earth's continents and oceans might have formed and changed over time. His evidence came from many fields of science. Wegener noted that the continental shelves fit together like the pieces of a puzzle. A **continental shelf** is the part of a continent that extends under shallow water from the ocean's edge down to a steeper slope. He noted that the fossil remains of certain species

of plants and animals were found on widely separated continents. The plants and animals that left these fossil remains could not have crossed the oceans.

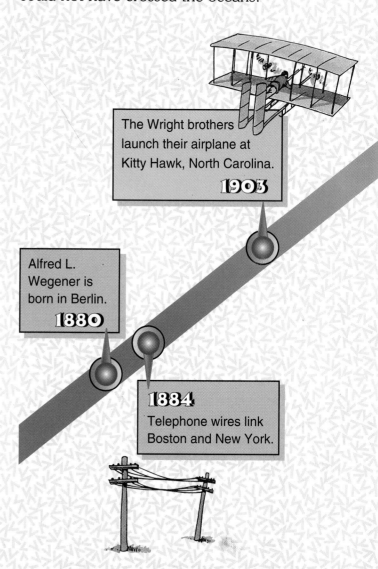

The Wright brothers launch their airplane at Kitty Hawk, North Carolina.
1903

Alfred L. Wegener is born in Berlin.
1880

1884
Telephone wires link Boston and New York.

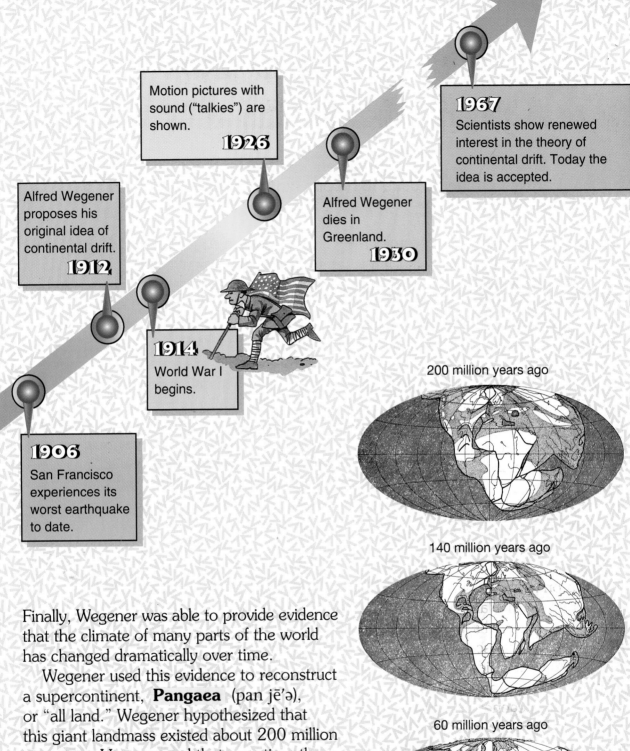

Motion pictures with sound ("talkies") are shown.
1926

1967
Scientists show renewed interest in the theory of continental drift. Today the idea is accepted.

Alfred Wegener proposes his original idea of continental drift.
1912

Alfred Wegener dies in Greenland.
1930

1914
World War I begins.

1906
San Francisco experiences its worst earthquake to date.

200 million years ago

140 million years ago

60 million years ago

Finally, Wegener was able to provide evidence that the climate of many parts of the world has changed dramatically over time.

Wegener used this evidence to reconstruct a supercontinent, **Pangaea** (pan jē′ə), or "all land." Wegener hypothesized that this giant landmass existed about 200 million years ago. He proposed that over time the landmass broke apart, and he concluded that the continents are still moving. Wegener's hypothesis on the movement of the continents is called continental drift. Despite all the evidence cited, it wasn't until the 1960s that scientists took Wegener's hypothesis seriously. ■

▲ **Wegener's maps of drifting continents**

B9

Evidence for Continental Drift

Reading Focus What evidence led Wegener to believe that Earth's continents used to be one landmass?

Alfred Wegener was a meteorologist—a scientist who studies weather. But he was interested in many fields of science. His **theory of continental drift** stated that the continents were once one landmass that had broken apart and moved to their present positions. This theory was supported by many pieces of evidence.

The Rock Record

In the activity on pages B6 and B7, the outlines of the continents seem to fit together like pieces of a jigsaw puzzle. This apparent fit was an important piece of evidence for Wegener's theory. He found that the continental shelves of Africa and South America fit together almost perfectly. In addition, many of the rocks that make up mountains in Argentina were identical to those found in South Africa. It seemed unlikely to Wegener that these identical rock layers were formed in such widely separated places at the same time.

By the time Wegener published the third edition of his book, he had discovered diamond-rich rocks in South Africa that were similar to rocks in Brazil. He also found that many of the coal beds in North America, Britain, and Belgium had been deposited in the same geological period. And a thick red sandstone layer crossed continental boundaries from North America to Greenland, Britain, and Norway. Look at the map shown below. What pieces of evidence can you name that support the theory of continental drift?

Using Math *Scientists think that South America and Africa were once joined. They estimate that the Atlantic Ocean formed at a rate of 2 cm to 4 cm a year for 200 million years. Estimate the width of the Atlantic Ocean today.*

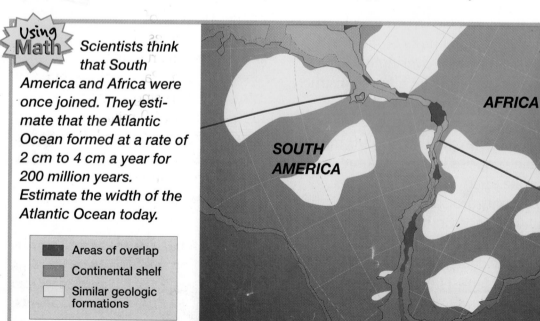

■ Areas of overlap
■ Continental shelf
□ Similar geologic formations

AFRICA

SOUTH AMERICA

The Fossil Record

Wegener also noted that certain fossils were preserved in rocks of the same age on different continents. He argued that the remains of these once-living organisms were so similar that they must have been left by the same kinds of organisms. One of these creatures was a small reptile called *Mesosaurus*, which had lived in fresh water. Other fossils found in rocks that were very far apart were those of the plant *Glossopteris*. Remains of the plant had been discovered in South America, Australia, Asia, and Africa. How, Wegener asked, could this plant have survived the different climates of these four landmasses?

Because of his training as a meteorologist, much of Wegener's evidence included information about climate. You probably already know that Earth can be divided into three major climate zones. The tropics are located near the equator and extend to about $23\frac{1}{2}°$ north and south of the equator. The temperate zones lie between the tropics and the polar zones. The polar climatic zones extend from about $66\frac{1}{2}°$ north and south to the poles.

Wegener noted that fossils of beech, maple, oak, poplar, ash, chestnut, and elm trees had been found on a small island named

◀ A variety of *Glossopteris*, a plant with fossil remains found in widely separated continents

Spitsbergen, near the North Pole. These trees generally grow only in temperate areas. Today, however, the island is covered for much of the year with snow and ice because it has a very cold climate —a polar climate.

Coal forms in swampy marshes that receive a lot of rain each year. Today coal beds are forming near the equator and in some temperate regions. Wegener proposed that coal beds in the eastern United States, Europe, and Siberia formed when the continents were joined and were located closer to the equator.

Another variety of *Glossopteris* ▼

Wegener used all of these different lines of evidence to reconstruct the supercontinent Pangaea. He hypothesized that this single landmass existed about 200 million years ago. Over time, he proposed, the landmass broke apart and the continents drifted to their present positions on Earth's surface. ∎

◀ Fossil remains of this reptile, *Mesosaurus*, were found on widely separated continents.

Continents on the Move

Reading Focus How did Pangaea break apart, and in what direction did its pieces move?

Wegener's hypothesis stated that Pangaea began to break apart about 180 million years ago. The smaller pieces of land drifted to their present position as Earth's continents. Although Wegener's idea was at first criticized, today it is accepted by scientists.

The maps on the next four pages show how landmasses—later Earth's continents—moved over time. Arrows on the continents show the direction in which they moved. Compare the location of the continents millions of years ago with their present location.

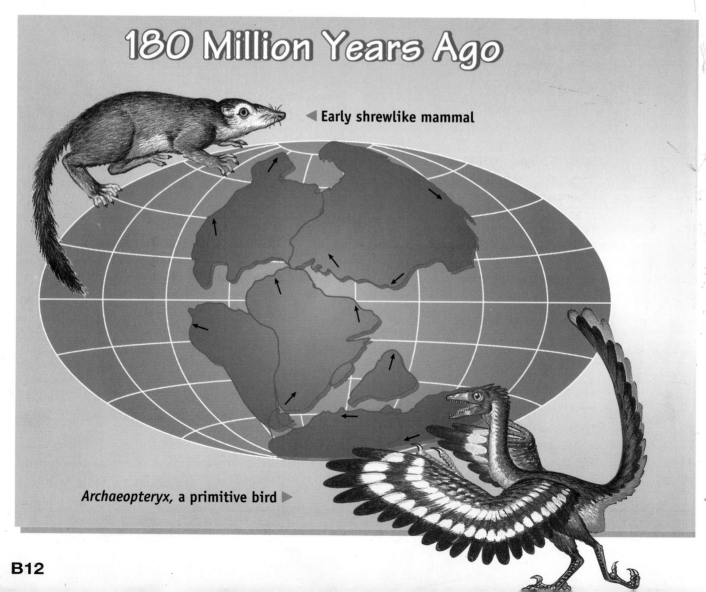

180 Million Years Ago

◄ Early shrewlike mammal

Archaeopteryx, a primitive bird ▶

135 Million Years Ago

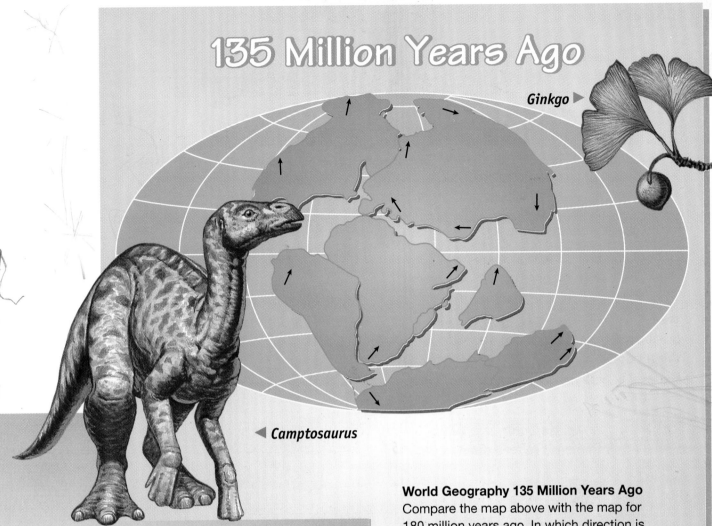

Ginkgo ▶

◀ Camptosaurus

World Geography 180 Million Years Ago
About 180 million years ago, North America, Europe, and much of Asia began to split from South America and Africa. India separated from the landmass around the South Pole and started moving northward. Australia and Antarctica drifted to the south and west. The Atlantic and Indian oceans began to form.

Life About 180 Million Years Ago
Green algae, corals, and sponges lived in the warm waters that covered much of Earth. Ammonites, which looked like giant snails, also inhabited Earth's oceans. Many amphibians, including ancestors of modern frogs, roamed the land. The first dinosaurs appeared on Earth. Somewhat later, *Archaeopteryx*, a birdlike animal, also lived on Earth. Conifers were the dominant plants.

World Geography 135 Million Years Ago
Compare the map above with the map for 180 million years ago. In which direction is North America moving? How does the location of India compare with that on the map for 180 million years ago? In which direction is Australia moving? What has happened to South America and Africa?

Life About 135 Million Years Ago
Sea urchins, sand dollars, and green algae populated the seas. Dinosaurs such as *Camptosaurus*, *Stegosaurus*, *Allosaurus*, and *Apatosaurus* roamed the land. Birds soared through the sky. Conifers, ferns, and ginkgoes made up the plant life on the planet.

65 Million Years Ago

World Geography 65 Million Years Ago

Although the map below shows Earth's landmasses 65 million years ago, it probably looks much more familiar to you than do the two maps on the previous pages. Describe how the locations of South America and Africa differ from their locations 135 million years ago. Describe the direction in which North America is moving. How far north has India moved as compared with its position 135 million years ago? Which two southern present-day continents are shown here still joined?

Life About 65 Million Years Ago

Fish, plankton, corals, and sponges were major forms of marine life. Insects were very abundant on land. These creatures pollinated the new flowering plants. *Ankylosaurus*, *Triceratops*, and *Tyrannosaurus* were some of the kinds of dinosaurs that lived at this time.

***Ankylosaurus*, a heavily plated dinosaur** ▶

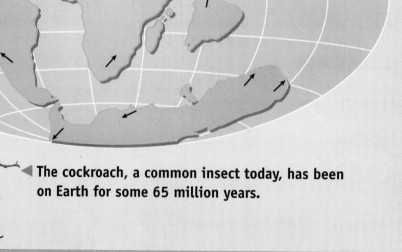

◀ **The cockroach, a common insect today, has been on Earth for some 65 million years.**

Today

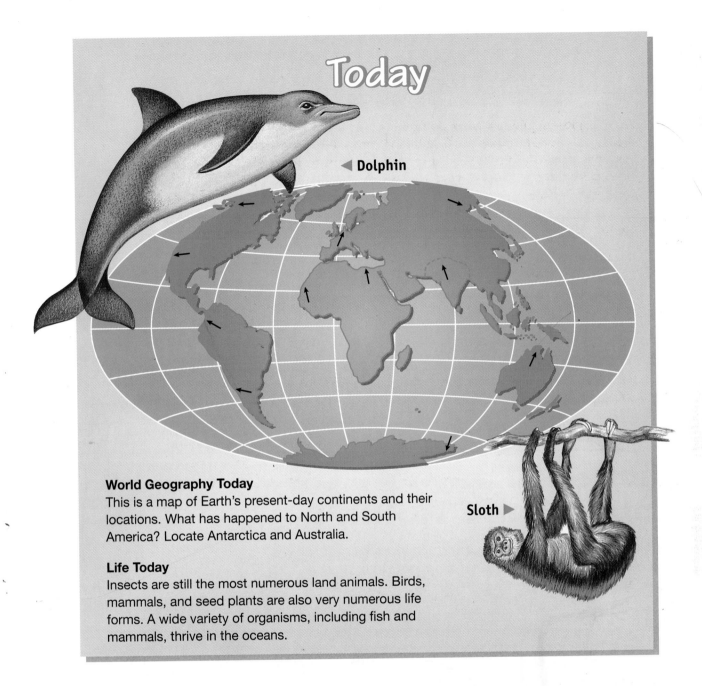

◄ **Dolphin**

Sloth ►

World Geography Today
This is a map of Earth's present-day continents and their locations. What has happened to North and South America? Locate Antarctica and Australia.

Life Today
Insects are still the most numerous land animals. Birds, mammals, and seed plants are also very numerous life forms. A wide variety of organisms, including fish and mammals, thrive in the oceans.

INVESTIGATION 1 WRAP-UP

REVIEW

1. What is Pangaea?

2. Describe some of the evidence Alfred Wegener used to show that the continents are moving.

CRITICAL THINKING

3. Evidence of glaciers has been found in southern Africa. What can you infer about where this continent may have been located in the past?

4. It is 1912 and you are Alfred Wegener. Write a short outline for your speech defining your ideas about moving continents.

INVESTIGATION ② WHAT DO THE LOCATIONS OF VOLCANOES AND EARTHQUAKES TELL US?

Earthquakes and volcanoes make our world a bit shaky! Think of all the stories you have heard about earthquakes and volcanic eruptions. Can the locations of these events give us clues about continental drift?

Activity

Earth—Always Rockin' and Rollin'!

Did you ever wonder why earthquakes occur where they do? See if you can find any pattern in the locations of earthquakes.

MATERIALS
- earthquake map of Earth
- tracing paper
- *Science Notebook*

How is Earth's crust like a cracked eggshell? ▼

Procedure

1. Study the earthquake map. Every dot on the map represents a place where a strong earthquake has occurred. Look for a pattern that the dots form. **Describe** this pattern in your *Science Notebook*. **Discuss** your observations with your team members.

2. On tracing paper, use your pencil to trace and then darken the pattern formed by the earthquake dots. Work with your team members to decide how to draw the pattern.

3. Think about the way a cracked eggshell looks. Earth's **crust**, which is its outermost, solid layer, is a lot like a cracked eggshell, broken up into large pieces. Look again at the pattern of the earthquake dots. How is the pattern of the dots like the cracks of an eggshell? **Record** your answer.

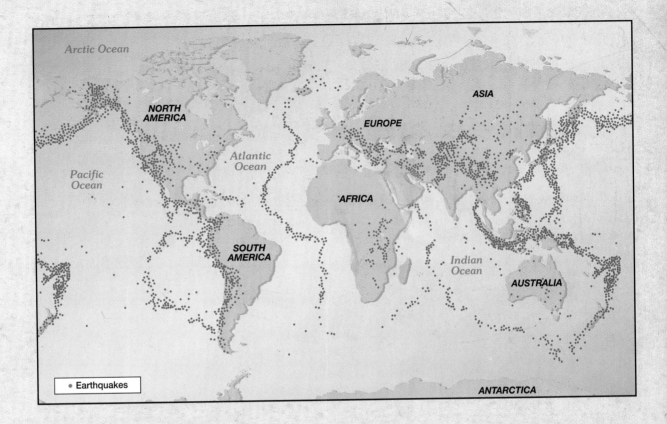

Arctic Ocean

NORTH
AMERICA

EUROPE

ASIA

Atlantic
Ocean

Pacific
Ocean

AFRICA

SOUTH
AMERICA

Indian
Ocean

AUSTRALIA

• Earthquakes

ANTARCTICA

Analyze and Conclude

1. Earth's crust is broken into large pieces called **tectonic plates**. Use your tracing and the map to locate some of these tectonic plates.

2. Earthquakes occur mostly along cracks in Earth's crust. **Predict** some locations where earthquakes are likely to occur. **Record** your predictions.

UNIT PROJECT LINK

For this Unit Project you will collect data about earthquakes and volcanic activity around the world. Then you will place map pins on a classroom map to show where this activity is taking place. Start by creating a map that shows the tectonic plate on which your town is located and the surrounding tectonic plate(s). Place a map pin to show the location of your town. If possible, determine how far your town is from the edge of a plate. Predict how likely your town is to have an earthquake.

Technology Link

For more help with your Unit Project, go to **www.eduplace.com**.

Activity

Volcanoes and Earth's Plates

Earthquakes occur at the edges of huge slabs of crust and upper mantle called tectonic plates. Do volcanoes and earthquakes occur in the same places?

MATERIALS
- map of Earth's volcanoes
- map of Earth's earth-quakes (page B17)
- *Science Notebook*

Arctic Ocean

Arctic Ocean

NORTH AMERICA

ASIA

EUROPE

Pacific Ocean

Atlantic Ocean

AFRICA

Pacific Ocean

SOUTH AMERICA

Indian Ocean

AUSTRALIA

▲ Volcanic Activity

ANTARCTICA

Procedure

Study the map of Earth's volcanoes and compare it with your map of Earth's earthquakes. In your *Science Notebook*, list the places where volcanoes occur.

Form a hypothesis about the locations of volcanoes, earthquakes, and the edges of Earth's tectonic plates. Record your hypothesis. Discuss your observations with your group.

Analyze and Conclude

1. Using the maps on pages B17 and B18, describe where both earthquakes and volcanoes occur.

2. How do the locations of earthquakes and volcanoes help identify Earth's tectonic plates?

Technology Link CD-ROM

INVESTIGATE FURTHER!

Use the **Science Processor CD-ROM**, *The Changing Earth* (Investigation 1, Map It!) to map earthquakes and volcanoes. Predict where future earthquakes and volcanoes will occur.

The Cracked Crust: Tectonic Plates

Reading Focus What are tectonic plates, and how do they help explain the drifting continents?

Sometimes you'll hear the expression "It's as solid as a rock." This expression means that whatever is referred to is permanent and dependable. We may like to think that rock is solid and permanent, but even large slabs of rock move. Actually, nothing on the surface of Earth is permanent. Even the continent of North America is moving very slowly. The slow movement of Earth's continents can be explained by the theory of plate tectonics.

Floating Plates

In the late 1960s, scientists expanded Alfred Wegener's idea of drifting continents and proposed the theory of plate tectonics. The word *tectonics* refers to the forces that cause the movement of Earth's rock formations and plates.

The **theory of plate tectonics** states that Earth's crust and upper mantle are broken into enormous slabs called plates or **tectonic plates**. (The **crust** is Earth's outermost, solid layer. The **mantle** is the layer of Earth between the crust and the core.) The plates are like enormous ships, and the continents are like their cargo. Scientists believe that currents in the plasticlike mantle cause the plates to move across Earth's surface. The currents are caused by differences in temperature in Earth's interior regions.

This theory has guided scientists in trying to figure out how Earth might have looked millions of years ago. Plate tectonics has helped them reconstruct the ways the continents might have moved over millions of years.

A wedge showing Earth's layers (*left*); a section of the crust and upper mantle (*right*).

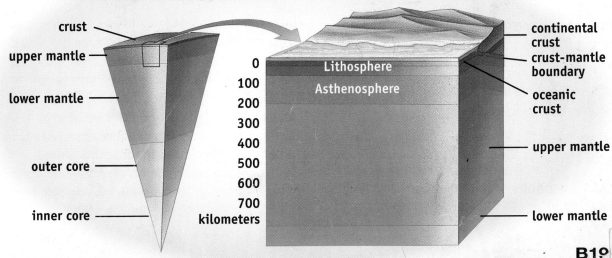

Makeup of the Plates

What do tectonic plates consist of? Each plate is formed of a thin layer of crust, which overlies a region called the upper mantle. In a plate that carries a continent, the crust can be 40 to 48 km (25 to 30 mi) thick. In a plate that is under an ocean, the crust may be only 5 to 8 km (3 to 5 mi) thick. The drawing below shows the makeup of part of two different tectonic plates.

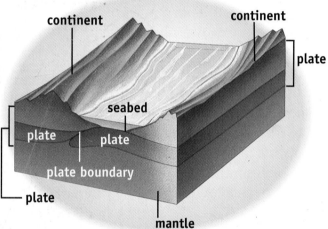

▲ Tectonic plates can carry a continent, an ocean, or both.

Interacting Plates

Plates can interact in three ways: (1) They can come together, (2) they can move apart, and (3) they can slide past one another. Places where plates interact are called **plate boundaries**. As you probably know by now, earthquakes and volcanoes occur along plate boundaries. In Chapter 2 you will find out much more about what happens along these boundaries. ■

Internet Field Trip

Visit **www.eduplace.com** to see an illustration of Earth's crust, mantle, and core.

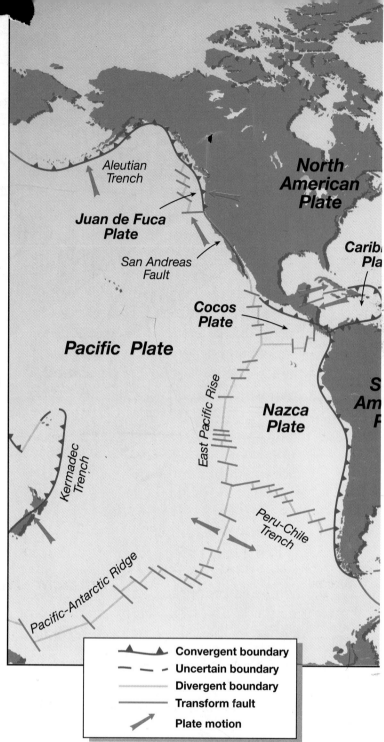

Legend:
- ▲‿▲ Convergent boundary
- – – – Uncertain boundary
- ——— Divergent boundary
- ——— Transform fault
- ➚ Plate motion

EARTH'S TECTONIC PLATES There are seven major plates and several minor ones. Many of the plates are named after the major landmasses that are parts of the plates. The plates act like ships that carry Earth's crust and upper mantle around on a layer of semisolid material. Observe that most of the United States is located on the North American Plate. In what direction is this plate moving? In what direction is the Pacific Plate moving?

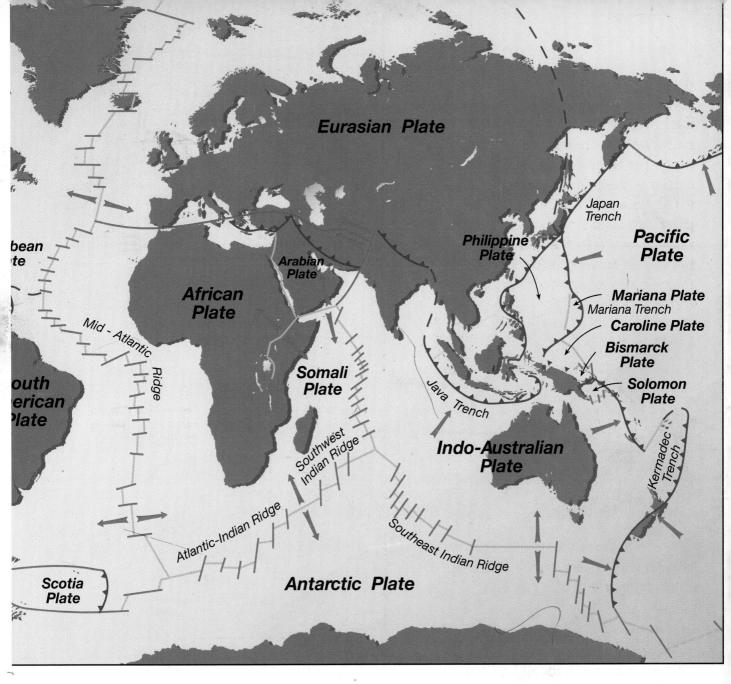

Eurasian Plate

Japan Trench

Pacific Plate

Philippine Plate

Mariana Plate
Mariana Trench

Caroline Plate

Bismarck Plate

Solomon Plate

Arabian Plate

African Plate

Mid - Atlantic Ridge

Somali Plate

Java Trench

Indo-Australian Plate

bean te

outh erican late

South American Plate

Southwest Indian Ridge

Atlantic-Indian Ridge

Southeast Indian Ridge

Kermadec Trench

Scotia Plate

Antarctic Plate

INVESTIGATION 2 WRAP-UP

REVIEW

1. Use the maps in this investigation to infer the connection between earthquakes, volcanoes, and plates.

2. What are the three ways that tectonic plates can interact?

CRITICAL THINKING

3. Suppose the Pacific Plate and the North American Plate continue moving in the directions they are now traveling. What might eventually happen to California's coastline?

4. Why is it unlikely that some of the tectonic plates will stop moving?

WHAT DOES THE SEA FLOOR TELL US ABOUT PLATE TECTONICS?

How do scientists know what the sea floor looks like? Is there evidence for plate tectonics hidden beneath the waters? Find out in this investigation.

Activity

Sea-Floor Spreading

New rock is being added to the sea floor all the time. Model this process in this activity.

MATERIALS
- sheet of paper with 3 slits, each 10 cm long
- 2 strips of notebook paper, each 9.5 × 27 cm long
- metric ruler
- scissors
- pencil
- *Science Notebook*

Procedure

Prepare a sheet of white paper as shown in the top drawing. Draw mountains along the sides. The middle slit represents a mid-ocean ridge, which is a very long crack in the ocean floor, with mountain ranges on either side.

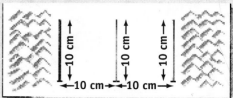

Pull two strips of notebook paper up through the middle slit and down through the side slits, as shown. These strips represent magma that is flowing up through the ocean ridge and then hardening. As you pull the strips, you **model** a process called sea-floor spreading.

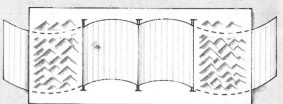

Analyze and Conclude

Consider that the magma coming up through the ridge is hardening into rock. What can you **infer** about the age of the rock along each side of the ridge? **Record** your ideas in your *Science Notebook.* Where on the sea floor do you think you would find the oldest rock?

Activity

Mapping the Ocean Floor

As on dry land, mountains, valleys, and plains exist on the ocean floor. You can model these structures and then model a way to map the sea floor.

MATERIALS
- clay
- shoebox
- pencil
- metric ruler
- tape
- plastic straw
- graph paper
- *Science Notebook*

Procedure

1. Use clay to **model** some sea-floor structures on the bottom of a shoebox. Use a pencil to punch a line of holes about 3 cm apart down the center of the lid. Number the holes in sequence and tape the lid onto the box. Exchange boxes with another team.

2. Insert a straw into a hole until it hits the "ocean floor." Remove the straw and **measure** the part of the straw that was beneath the lid. This measurement represents the depth of the "ocean" at that hole. Repeat for each hole. **Record** the depths in your *Science Notebook.*

3. **Make a line graph** of your results. The vertical axis should be *below* the horizontal axis. Show depth on the vertical axis and distance on the horizontal axis.

> See **SCIENCE** and **MATH TOOLBOX** page H6 if you need to review **Making a Line Graph.**

Step 2

Analyze and Conclude

1. What does the lid of the shoebox represent?

2. Remove the lid and **compare** your graph to the "ocean floor." Does your graph resemble the clay model?

B23

Sonar: Mapping the Sea Floor

Reading Focus How do scientists use sound to make a map of the ocean floor?

In the activity on page B23, a shoebox, clay, and straws are used as a crude model of sonar—a method for finding the shape and depth of the ocean floor. *Sonar* stands for "**so**und **na**vigation and **r**anging."

Listening for Echoes

British naval scientists first developed sonar in 1921. During World War II (1939–1945), sonar was used to detect enemy submarines. Scientists realized that sound could be used to measure the distance from a ship on the surface of the water to the bottom of the ocean.

A sonar device sends out a sound and then listens for an echo to return. By using sonar, scientists can measure the time between sending out a sound and receiving the echo of that sound. Then, by knowing this time and the speed at

which sound travels through sea water, they can compute the depth of the ocean at that point. In the activity "Mapping the Ocean Floor," a straw pushed through the holes in a shoebox lid represent sound impulses sent out from a sonar device.

Mapping by Sound

As a ship with sonar moves along the surface of the ocean, it sends out sound impulses. The impulses travel down through the sea water, strike the ocean

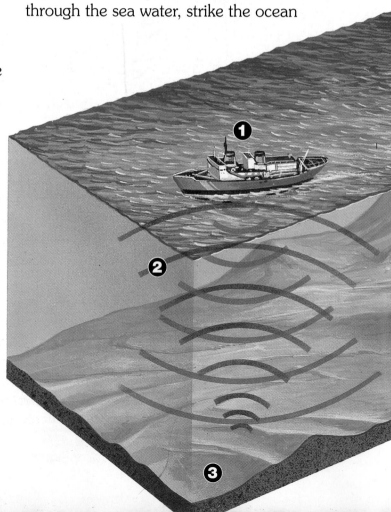

Mapping With Sonar

  Ship sends out sound impulses from sonar device. Impulses travel at a rate of 5,130 m/s.

 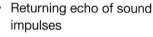 Returning echo of sound impulses

  Sea floor

floor, and then bounce back as an echo. Each echo arrives at a receiver back at the ship and is recorded on a recording chart. The sonar device records the length of time required for the impulse to travel to the ocean floor and for the echo to return to the ship. It then computes the depth of the ocean floor at that point, which is registered on a scale.

Suppose the total time for a sound to travel from the ship to the ocean floor and back is 6.60 s. Since sound travels through sea water at 1,530 m/s, the sound has traveled a total of 10,098 m. The distance from the ship to the ocean floor is half the total, or 5,049 m. By assembling all the measurements taken as the ship moves through the water,

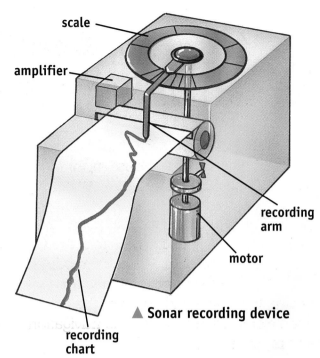

▲ **Sonar recording device**

scientists can produce a map of a section of the ocean floor. The more readings they take, the more accurate their map will be.

Sonar has allowed scientists to discover many new features of the ocean floor. For example, they have found some places that are over 10,600 m (6.3 mi) deep. That's over 10 km! They also have found undersea mountains higher than the highest mountain on the surface, Mount Everest, which is 8,848 m (29,198 ft) high!

Sonar can also be used on land. Sound pulses can be sent through the ground, and the returning echoes can be used to identify different layers of soil and rock as well as to locate deposits of natural gas and oil. ■

Using Math *The* Titanic *lies about 4,000 m (13,200 ft) below the ocean's surface. About how long would it take a sound impulse to travel from a ship at the ocean's surface to the* Titanic *and back to the ship?*

Magnetism Tells a Story

Reading Focus How is Earth like a magnet?

You have probably used magnets many times. Perhaps you used one to pick up a string of paper clips or to hold notes on the refrigerator door.

A magnet is an object that attracts certain metals, including iron, steel, and nickel. A magnet has two ends, or poles. When a magnet is suspended from a

inclined, or tilted, about 11° from the geographic poles. The magnetic field around Earth is thought to be due to movements within Earth's fluid outer core, which is composed mainly of iron and nickel. For reasons unknown, Earth's magnetic field sometimes reverses itself. This is called a **magnetic reversal**.

▲ Iron filings show the magnetic field around a magnet.

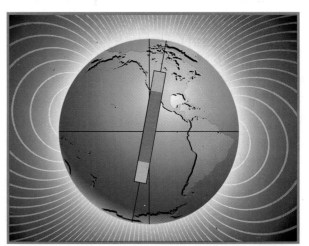

▲ Earth is like a giant magnet surrounded by a magnetic field.

string, the pole that turns toward north is called the *north pole* of the magnet. The pole that points south is the *south pole* of the magnet. A **magnetic field** is the area around a magnet where the effects of magnetism are felt.

Earth as a Magnet

Earth is like a giant magnet, and it has two magnetic poles. These poles are

At present, the magnetic field is said to be normal. This means that the north-seeking needle of a compass will point toward Earth's north magnetic pole. What do you think happens when the field is reversed?

You probably know that some of Earth's rocks contain iron. When these rocks formed from magma, the iron atoms lined up with the magnetic field of the time, much as a compass needle lines up with Earth's magnetic field. Scientists can use this lining-up of iron atoms to find the direction of Earth's magnetic field at the time the rock formed.

Scientists use a device called a magnetometer (mag nə täm'ət ər) to detect how iron atoms line up within rock. These devices have been used by oceanographers to study the magnetic fields of rock on the ocean floor.

Sea-Floor Magnetism

A **mid-ocean ridge** is a continuous chain of mountains on the ocean floor. When scientists studied the ocean floor along these ridges and on either side of the ridges, they found a magnetic pattern in the rock. There were long stretches of rock in which iron atoms were lined up in one direction. Then there were other stretches of rock, parallel to the first, in which the iron particles lined up in the reverse direction. This pattern of reversals continued from the mid-ocean ridge outward, away from the ridge. A further finding was that the pattern on one side of the ridge was exactly the same as the pattern on the other side of the ridge.

The drawing below helps explain the magnetic patterns on the ocean floor. As tectonic plates on either side of the ridge move apart, magma flows up from below the ridge and hardens into rock on the sea floor. Only when iron-containing rock is fluid can the iron atoms line up in a magnetic field. Once the rock hardens, the iron atoms do not change direction. The arrows show the magnetic directions of the iron atoms in the rock at the mid-ocean ridge and on either side of the ridge. Note the repeating pattern.

Scientists have found that rocks closer to a mid-ocean ridge are younger than rocks farther from the ridge. The magnetic patterns in the sea-floor rocks and the different ages of the rocks led scientists to a startling conclusion. New sea floor is continually being formed along underwater mountain chains, or mid-ocean ridges! As two plates separate along a ridge, magma fills the separation.

SEA-FLOOR SPREADING Magma bubbles up and flows out along the ridge. When it hardens, it forms rock. On either side of a mid-ocean ridge are layers of magnetized rock. Each arrow represents a magnetic reversal. ▼

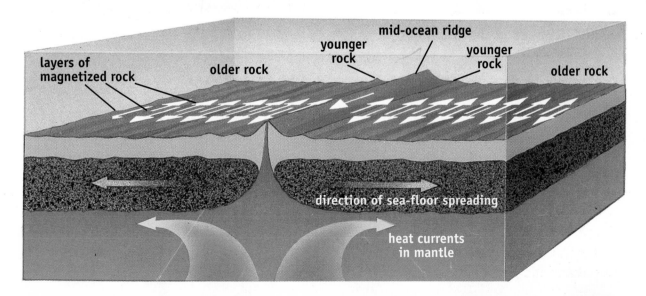

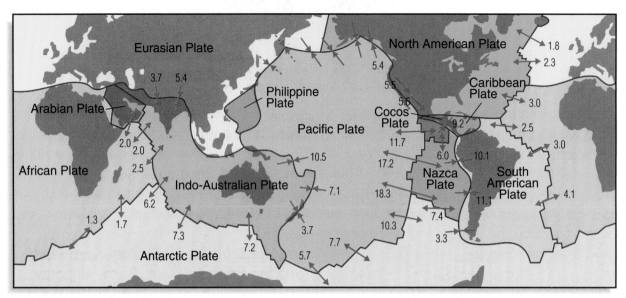

This map shows rates at which plates separate and move together. The rates are in centimeters per year. Where is sea-floor spreading taking place the fastest? Where is it occuring the slowest?

As the magma cools, the iron atoms in the magma line up with Earth's magnetic field. This process by which new ocean floor is continually being added is called **sea-floor spreading**. The activity on page B22 involves a model of sea-floor spreading. Sea-floor spreading is strong evidence for the plate tectonics theory. ■

Science in Literature

THE LONGEST FOUR MINUTES

"The earthquake lasted for four minutes, during which time the shocks set off avalanches and landslides . . . buildings rocked back and forth, while large cracks opened in the ground and swallowed objects as large as cars. On Turn Again Heights, the whole area slid more than 1,640 ft (500 m) . . . ."

In *Volcanoes and Earthquakes* by Basil Booth, you can read more about the 1964 earthquake that struck Prince William Sound in Alaska. You can also read about volcanoes and other famous earthquakes.

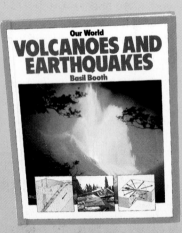

Volcanoes and Earthquakes
by Basil Booth
Silver Burdett Press, 1991

Heating Up Iceland

Reading Focus How can the movement of Earth's plates help produce energy, and what can that energy be used for?

In Iceland, some families don't need ovens to bake their bread; they simply place the dough inside a hole in the ground. Do they have underground ovens? Yes, but these ovens are created by natural processes taking place inside Earth. Rocks just below the surface are heated by magma that rises from deep inside Earth. Icelanders use these heated rocks as underground ovens.

Why It Is Hot

Iceland lies on the Mid-Atlantic Ridge, which marks the boundaries of two tectonic plates—the North American Plate and the Eurasian Plate. As these plates move apart, the heat produced by rising magma creates giant geysers. The drawing below shows how this happens.

Helpful Shifting Plates

The movement of Earth's plates can cause trouble. Earthquakes and volcanic eruptions often occur along the edges of moving plates. But there are regions where plate movement can be helpful. In Iceland, for example, moving plates provide an inexpensive source of energy—geothermal ("hot earth") energy.

A geothermal plant in Iceland ▼

GEYSERS Hot magma rises from inside Earth, heating the underground rock. The heated rock in turn heats any nearby ground water, changing it to steam. Some of this steam and heated water spurts out of the ground in the form of huge geysers. ▼

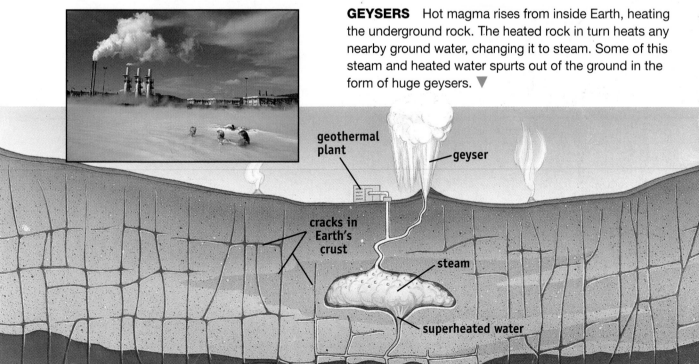

geothermal plant

geyser

cracks in Earth's crust

steam

superheated water

heated rock

Energy From Earth

Icelanders use this heated underground water as geothermal energy. This energy, which comes from heat produced inside Earth, is used by Icelanders to heat their homes, businesses, swimming pools, and greenhouses. The steam produced by the heated water runs generators that produce electrical energy.

Value of Geothermal Energy

Compared to other forms of energy, geothermal energy has many advantages, as you can see in the table below. Which form of energy is used where you live?

Geothermal energy is used in several parts of the world besides Iceland, such as in Italy, Japan, Australia, New Zealand, Russia, and the United States. Some of the same processes that can lead to a volcanic eruption can also be turned to useful purposes. The use of geothermal energy in Iceland shows that processes inside Earth can provide people with the heat and electricity they need every day. ■

Comparison of Forms of Energy

Energy	Advantages	Disadvantages
Fossil fuels	fairly plentiful	nonrenewable, polluting
Geothermal	less polluting than fossil fuels or nuclear energy	produces sulfur, boron, and ammonia wastes
Hydroelectric	cheap form of energy; renewable, nonpolluting	dams cause flooding of valuable land
Nuclear	cheap, powerful	toxic waste; risk of radiation leaks
Solar	renewable, nonpolluting	expensive development and maintenance

INVESTIGATION 3 WRAP-UP

REVIEW

1. What features might be found along the sea floor that could help us understand plate tectonics?

2. Explain how scientists use sonar to map the sea floor.

CRITICAL THINKING

3. You are planning a documentary film about the mysteries of the sea. How would you explain sea-floor spreading to your viewers?

4. You have just invented something that will make mapping the sea floor easier. Draw a diagram or write a paragraph explaining how your invention works.

REFLECT & EVALUATE

Word Power

Write the letter of the term that best matches the definition. *Not all terms will be used*.

1. Part of a continent that extends under shallow water from the edge of the land down to a steeper slope
2. Process by which new ocean floor is continually added
3. Supercontinent that existed 200 million years ago
4. Places where plates interact
5. Earth's outermost solid layer
6. Area around a magnet where effects of magnetism are felt

a. continental shelf
b. crust
c. magnetic field
d. magnetic reversal
e. mantle
f. Pangaea
g. plate boundaries
h. sea-floor spreading

Check What You Know

Write the word in each pair that correctly completes each sentence.

1. Wegener hypothesized that Pangaea existed about 200 (thousand, million) years ago.
2. Rocks close to a mid-ocean ridge are (younger, older) than rocks farther from the ridge.
3. The movement of Earth's continents can be explained by (magnetic reversal, the theory of plate tectonics).

Problem Solving

1. Careful measurements along the Mid-Atlantic Ridge show that South America is moving away from Africa at about 3 to 5 cm each year. How would you explain this?
2. Explain how the same kinds of rock could be found in Norway, Scotland, and parts of eastern Canada and the eastern United States.

BUILD YOUR PORTFOLIO

The map shows the location of earthquakes and volcanoes world-wide. Explain in your own words why there are so many earthquakes and volcanoes located in coastal areas that border the Pacific Ocean.

CHAPTER 2

TECTONIC PLATES AND MOUNTAINS

The Himalayas, the Andes, and other great mountain ranges have existed for millions of years. The largest of all mountain ranges is actually beneath an ocean. How do mountains form? Do mountains on land and beneath the ocean form in the same way?

Connecting to Science
CULTURE

The High Life The type of culture that develops in a region is greatly influenced by the geography of the region. No place on Earth is this fact more evident than in the Andes Mountains, which stretch along much of the west coast of South America. For people in the Andean highlands, life is much the same as it was for their Inca ancestors more than 500 years ago. The homes and clothing are designed to withstand the rugged conditions of the region. The main industry is farming. The chief crop is potatoes, which grow well in the thin soils and cool climate. Sheep, llamas, and alpacas are raised for their wool. Plant dyes are used to create beautifully bright patterns on blankets and other wool products. And as the picture shows, the goods are displayed and sold in colorful outdoor markets.

▲ Marketplace in Pisac, Peru.

WHY DO TECTONIC PLATES MOVE?

Wegener's hypothesis on continental drift helped to explain why the continents appear to be just so many pieces of a jigsaw puzzle. However, his hypothesis didn't explain why the continents moved. What force can move such huge plates of rock?

Activity

The Conveyor

Heat is a form of energy. Energy can do work. How can heat energy from Earth's interior move tectonic plates? In this activity you'll construct a model that shows what moves tectonic plates.

MATERIALS
- aquarium
- cold water
- milk carton (0.24 L)
- 2 lengths of string (30 cm each)
- duct tape
- measuring cup
- hot water
- food coloring
- scissors
- metric ruler
- paper towels
- *Science Notebook*

Procedure

1. Fill an aquarium with cold water.

2. Punch a 5-mm hole in the side of a milk carton, near the bottom. Punch another hole near the top of the carton.

3. Place a length of string over the hole near the bottom so that it extends down 2.5 cm below the hole. Cover the string and hole securely with a strip of duct tape, as shown.

4. Repeat step 3, this time covering the hole near the top of the carton.

Step 3

5. Using a measuring cup, fill the milk carton with hot water colored with food coloring. Seal the carton with duct tape.

6. Place the carton in the middle of the aquarium. Predict what will happen when the holes in the carton are opened. Record your predictions in your *Science Notebook*.

7. Have one group member hold down the milk carton while another member gently pulls the strings to peel the tape off the holes. Be careful not to stir up the water as you work. Watch what happens. Record your observations.

8. Form a hypothesis on how the movement in the aquarium is a model of the movement of material in Earth's crust and upper mantle. Discuss your hypothesis with your group.

Analyze and Conclude

1. What happened in step 7 when you removed the tape from the holes?

2. Did the hot water do what you predicted it would do? Compare your predictions with what actually happened.

3. If the hot and cold water represent the layer of Earth known as the mantle, which is just below the crust, how might material in the mantle move tectonic plates?

 Technology Link
CD-ROM
INVESTIGATE FURTHER!

Use the **Science Processor CD-ROM**, *The Changing Earth* (Unit Opener Investigation, On the Edge) to observe several earthquakes and volcanic eruptions. Find out about how tectonic plates interact and what makes plate boundaries so important.

Moving Plates

Reading Focus What force makes the tectonic plates move and how does this force work?

Recall from Chapter 1 that Earth's crust and upper mantle are broken into seven large slabs and several small ones. The slabs are called tectonic plates. These plates move over Earth's surface an average of several centimeters a year. Just what keeps these enormous slabs in motion?

Earth's Lithosphere

Tectonic plates make up a part of Earth called the lithosphere. The word part *litho-* means "rock." You probably know that *sphere* means "ball."

The **lithosphere** (lith'ō sfir), then, is the solid, rocky layer of Earth. It is about 100 km (62 mi) thick. This part of Earth includes the crust, with the oceans and continents, and the rigid upper mantle.

The layer of Earth below the lithosphere is the **asthenosphere** (as then'ə sfir). Unlike the lithosphere, the asthenosphere is not rigid. In fact, the part of the asthenosphere just below the lithosphere behaves something like silicon putty.

Silicon putty has properties of both a liquid and a solid. When a slow, steady force is applied to the putty, it flows like a thick liquid. However, when a quick, sharp force is applied to the putty, it snaps like a solid.

Pulling slowly on silicon putty (*left*)
Giving silicon putty a sharp tug (*right*)

Layers of Earth's crust and upper mantle ▼

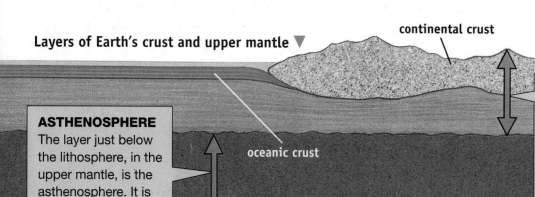

continental crust

ASTHENOSPHERE
The layer just below the lithosphere, in the upper mantle, is the asthenosphere. It is made up of rock that is hot, soft, and slightly fluid.

oceanic crust

LITHOSPHERE
Earth's rigid outer layer is the lithosphere. It includes the crust and solid upper part of the mantle.

Temperature increases steadily as you move deeper into the asthenosphere. In the lower part of the asthenosphere, temperatures are so high that the rock is partially melted. This mixture of molten and solid rock material behaves something like a very thick, very slow-moving syrup.

Convection currents in a pot of boiling pasta ▼

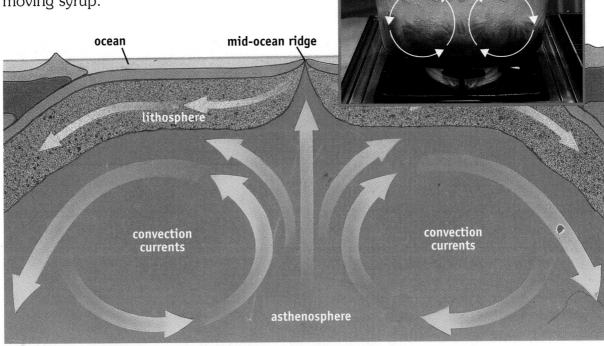

ocean   mid-ocean ridge

lithosphere

convection currents

convection currents

asthenosphere

▲ Convection currents in the asthenosphere are thought to drive the movement of the tectonic plates.

Heating and Cooling Rock

Scientists think that Earth's plates move over its surface because of convection in the asthenosphere. **Convection** (kən vek′shən) is a process by which heat energy is transferred through a fluid. Convection occurs when a fluid is placed between a hot surface below and a cold surface above. A **convection current** is the path along which the energy is transferred.

You are probably familiar with several kinds of convection currents. Have you ever watched rice or pasta whirl around in a pot of boiling water? Convection currents are set in motion when water or air is heated. The heated fluid then rises because it is less dense than the surrounding fluid. In a pot of rice or pasta, when the heated water reaches the top of the pot, it cools and flows back down to begin another journey around the pot. In the activity on pages B34 and B35, when the hot water in the milk carton is released into the colder water in the aquarium, convection currents are set into motion.

Convection in the Mantle

How does convection occur in Earth's mantle? The partly melted hot rock in the asthenosphere rises because it is less dense than the surrounding materials. It slowly makes its way toward the lithosphere. When the melted rock reaches the cooler lithosphere, the melted rock begins to cool and harden. The cooler rock then moves horizontally along the bottom of the lithosphere. When the rock reaches the edge of a plate, it sinks down under the plate into the mantle. As the rock moves down into the asthenosphere, it begins to melt, and the cycle starts again.

Moving Tectonic Plates

Today scientists generally agree that convection currents in the asthenosphere are the force that moves tectonic plates. Recall from Chapter 1 that Alfred Wegener, despite all his evidence, could

How Plates Interact

Places where plates interact are called plate boundaries Examples of three kinds of interacting plates are shown on this page and the next. The map on pages B20–B21 shows the location of these boundaries.

COLLIDING PLATES Plates collide, or come together, at **convergent boundaries**. What do you think might happen when two enormous slabs of rock collide? What kinds of features do you think you'll find along convergent boundaries?

▲ **Colliding plates**

SEPARATING PLATES Plates move away from one another at **divergent boundaries**. Most divergent boundaries are found on the ocean floor. These boundaries are places where new oceanic crust forms through the process of sea-floor spreading. The photograph shows a divergent boundary.

▲ **The walls of this riverbank in Iceland are on plates that separated.**

not explain what caused the continents to move over Earth's surface. Thus, his idea of continental drift was really a hypothesis, or a guess based on observations. In the 1960s the theory of plate tectonics was proposed. A theory is an idea that is supported by evidence. And a theory can be used to make accurate predictions about future events. Recall that the theory of plate tectonics states that Earth's crust and upper mantle are made up of a series of rigid or nearly rigid plates that are in motion. ■

Internet Field Trip

Visit **www.eduplace.com** to see animations of the three types of movement between plates.

SLIDING PLATES Plates move past one another at **transform-fault boundaries**. A fault is a very large crack in Earth's rocks, along which movement has taken place. The photograph shows the San Andreas Fault, found in the western United States. This fault, one of the longest and most famous in the world, is the site of many earthquakes.

▲ San Andreas Fault, California, as seen from an airplane

INVESTIGATION 1 WRAP-UP

THINK IT WRITE IT

REVIEW

1. What might cause tectonic plates to move?

2. Explain the convection currents in a pot of boiling pasta.

CRITICAL THINKING

3. Can convergent and divergent plate boundaries be considered opposites? Explain.

4. What do you suppose would happen if Earth's tectonic plates began moving at a much faster rate, such as several meters per year instead of centimeters per year?

HOW DOES THE MOTION OF TECTONIC PLATES BUILD MOUNTAINS?

The tectonic plates that make up Earth's surface are large, thick, and massive. When they move, something has to give! Find out what "gives" in Investigation 2.

Activity

Take a Dive

Some plates are thicker than others and some bend easier than others. What do you think happens when an ocean plate collides with a continental plate?

Procedure

1. Turn a shoebox lid upside down. Make a slit from one side of the lid to the other about 1 cm from one end of the lid.

2. Cut a sheet of paper to form a strip several cm longer than the box lid and about 2 cm narrower. Lay it inside the lid. Then sprinkle a thin layer of rice on the paper.

3. The paper represents the plate that is the ocean floor. The end of the box near the slit is a continent. The slit is an ocean trench next to the continent. The rice is a layer of sediment on the ocean floor. **Predict** what will happen when you pull the paper through the slit.

Step 2

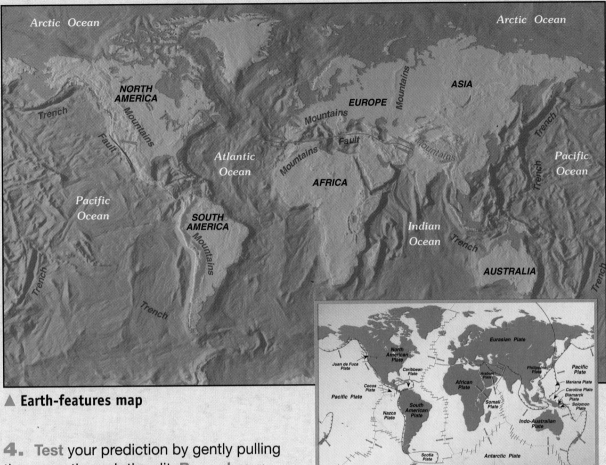

▲ **Earth-features map**

▲ **Tectonic-plates map. For the full-size map, see pages B20 and B21.**

4. Test your prediction by gently pulling the paper through the slit. Record your observations in your *Science Notebook*.

5. Form a hypothesis about what happens when two plates meet at a convergent boundary.

Analyze and Conclude

1. How does the model show what happens as ocean plates collide with continental plates?

2. What happens to sediment on an ocean plate when the plate descends beneath a continent? Infer what all this sediment might build.

UNIT PROJECT LINK

After several earthquakes shook California in the 1990s, the Sierra Nevada range became more than 0.3 m (1 ft) taller. Use newspapers and magazines to find out about earthquakes and volcanoes that have recently lifted other mountains. Use a map to identify the locations of the growing mountains.

TechnologyLink For more help with your Unit Project, go to **www.eduplace.com**.

Activity

A Big Fender Bender

Think about what happens to the metal when two cars collide. What do you think happens when two continents collide? You'll use a simple model to find out.

MATERIALS
- shoebox lid
- paper strip
- block of wood
- rice
- colored beans or peas
- *Science Notebook*

Procedure

1. Use the shoebox lid and paper strip from the last activity. Tape a block of wood to the end of the paper strip farthest from the slit in the lid. The block represents a continent.

2. Build a second model continent on the paper strip in front of the wood block. Use rice and colored beans or peas to represent layers of rock.

3. Predict what will happen when you pull the model ocean floor down into the "trench" so that the continents collide. Test your prediction. Record your observations in your *Science Notebook*.

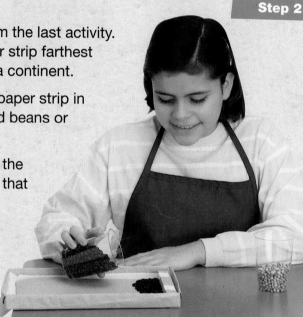

Step 2

Analyze and Conclude

1. What happened to the "layers of rock" on the continent?

2. Infer what happens to actual rock when continents collide. Hypothesize about the relationship between Earth's tectonic plates and mountains.

Technology Link
CD-ROM

INVESTIGATE FURTHER!

Use the **Science Processor CD-ROM**, *The Changing Earth* (Investigation 2, On the Move) to learn how plate movements affect the way that mountains form.

Mountain Building

Reading Focus What are the four different ways that mountains are formed?

Have you ever gone mountain climbing? A mountain is any feature that rises above the surrounding landscape. So even if you've only hiked a local hill, you've gone mountain climbing.

Mountains form as the result of four basic processes: folding, faulting, doming, and volcanic activity—so mountains can be classified as folded mountains, fault-block mountains, dome mountains, or volcanoes. Three of these—folded, fault-block, and volcanic—result from plate movements.

Folded Mountains

Look at the picture of the paper fan at the bottom of this page. Notice that the folds form a series of crests, or high points, and troughs, or low points. Folded mountains form when masses of rock are squeezed from opposite sides. The activities on pages B40 to B42 show that folded mountains form when two plates collide. The Appalachians, the Alps, the Urals, and the Himalayas are classified as folded mountains.

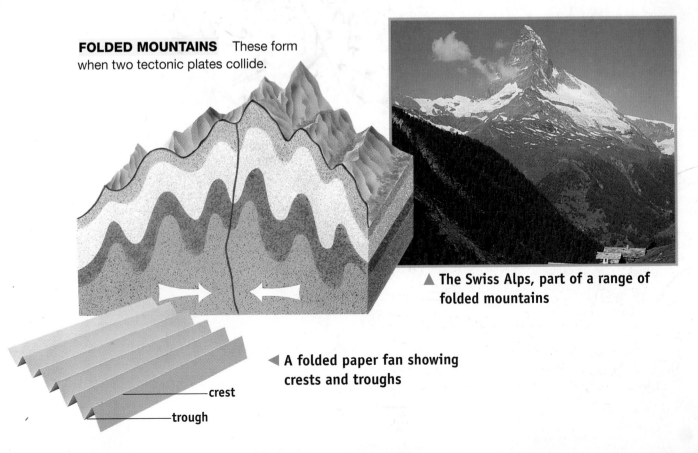

FOLDED MOUNTAINS   These form when two tectonic plates collide.

▲ The Swiss Alps, part of a range of folded mountains

◄ A folded paper fan showing crests and troughs

crest

trough

Fault-Block Mountains

Recall that a fault is a large crack in Earth's rocks, along which movement has taken place. Forces produced by moving plates can move rock along faults. When blocks of rock move up or down along a fault, a mountain can form.

Examples of fault-block mountains include those in the Dead Sea area, the Grand Tetons in Wyoming, and those in the Great Rift Valley of Africa. In the mountains of the Great Rift Valley, scientists have unearthed some of the oldest known human fossils.

Dome Mountains

Have you ever heard of Pikes Peak? This granite summit in the Colorado Rockies is 4,341 m (14,110 ft) tall. It was explored in 1806 by Zebulon Pike. Although the peak was eventually named after him, Pike never even reached its summit! Pikes Peak is a dome mountain that formed millions of years ago when forces deep within Earth pushed magma toward the surface, where it cooled and hardened. Although dome mountains have an igneous core, sedimentary rocks can border such mountains. But erosion often strips away the sedimentary rocks to reveal the harder igneous core.

Other dome mountains in the United States include the Sangre de Cristo Mountains, the Bighorn Mountains, the Black Hills, and Longs Peak. Find these dome mountains on a map of the United States. Are any of them in your state or in nearby states?

Science in Literature

THE BIG SQUEEZE

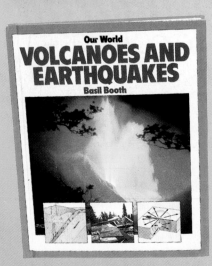

Volcanoes and Earthquakes
by Basil Booth
Silver Burdett Press, 1991

"Mountain chains are formed when two continents collide. . . . Rock debris eroded from these colliding continents pours into the trenches where the oceanic plate is being destroyed. This adds to the ocean floor material to form thick sediments. When the two continents eventually meet, the sediments are folded and squeezed up, like putty in a vice. This creates mountains, such as the Alps and the Himalayas."

Read more about the formation of mountains in *Volcanoes and Earthquakes* by Basil Booth.

FAULT-BLOCK MOUNTAINS These mountains form when masses of rock move up or down along a fault.

▲ Wasatch Range, Utah, fault-block mountains

DOME MOUNTAINS These mountains form when the surface is lifted up by magma, forming a broad dome, or bulge. Wind and rain erode the dome, stripping away layers of sedimentary rock and exposing the igneous rock below.

▲ Pikes Peak, Colorado, a dome mountain

INVESTIGATE FURTHER!

EXPERIMENT

Use a few different colors of modeling clay to demonstrate how folded mountains form. Then use the clay and a plastic knife to show how fault-block mountains form. USE CARE IN HANDLING THE KNIFE. Make sketches of your models in your *Science Notebook*.

Volcanoes

Have you ever opened a bottle of warm soda and had it spray all over you? The spraying of the soda is a bit like the eruption of magma when a volcano forms. Volcanoes, a fourth type of mountain, are most common along convergent and divergent plate boundaries. They form when magma, or molten rock, erupts from an opening in Earth's surface. Sometimes the eruption is quiet; at other times it is quite forceful.

Mount St. Helens is a volcano in the Cascade Range. This mountain chain extends from northern California to British Columbia, in Canada. On May 18, 1980, Mount St. Helens blew its top and threw dust, ash, and volcanic rocks more than 18,000 m (60,000 ft) into the air! As the ash rained back down to Earth, it blanketed some places with as much as 2 m (6.6 ft) of fine material. In some places the air was so thick with ash that it looked like midnight when it was actually noon! You will learn much more about different kinds of volcanoes and volcanic cones in Chapter 4. ■

Mount St. Helens, Washington, before the 1980 eruption (*top*); during the eruption (*middle*); and after the eruption (*bottom*).

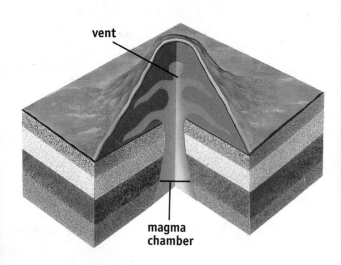

vent

magma chamber

▲ A typical volcano

Life at the Top

Reading Focus Why is living at high altitudes a problem, and what adaptation helps people deal with the problem?

You now know that folded mountains are formed by the interactions of tectonic plates. The Himalaya Mountains, for example, were formed millions of years ago when the plate carrying India, then a separate continent, rammed into the plate carrying Asia. This enormous collision of plates crumpled the crust and lifted up sediment from the ocean floor, forming the Himalayas. In some places the sediment was raised up thousands of meters, forming folded mountains.

Climbers of very high mountains can experience many difficulties. The lower air pressure at higher altitudes means that less oxygen is taken in with each breath. A lack of oxygen can affect vision and make walking dangerous. Heart rate quickens sharply, and the heart tries to supply more oxygen to the body.

People in Nepal, a country in the Himalayas, have adapted to living high

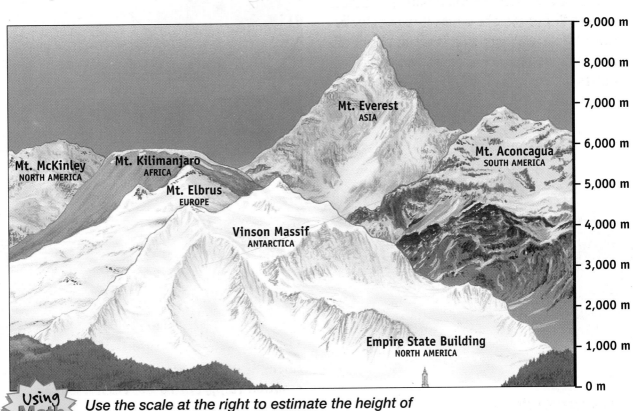

Use the scale at the right to estimate the height of each of the world's highest mountains.

▲ Tenzing Norgay climbed Mount Everest.

▲ Sherpa women in their mountain village

up in the mountains. Nepal is the home of the highest mountain peak in the world—Mount Everest, which towers 8,848 m (29,028 ft) above sea level.

The Sherpas, a people of Tibetan ancestry who live mainly in Nepal, are known for their ability to live and work in the high terrain of their country.

Because the Sherpas have lived all their lives in the mountains, their blood contains more oxygen-carrying red blood cells than that of most other people. So, with each breath the Sherpas take, they can absorb more available oxygen and pump it throughout their bodies. The ability to move enough oxygen through-out the body prevents many problems. In fact, Tenzing Norgay, a Sherpa, was one of the first two men to climb to the top of Mount Everest!

Visitors to the high mountains adapt to the lower air pressure after several weeks. What happens? Like the bodies of the native peoples, their bodies produce more of the oxygen-carrying red blood cells. In time, newcomers to the high mountains can also pump more oxygen throughout their bodies. ■

INVESTIGATION 2 WRAP-UP

REVIEW

1. Describe how plate movements contribute to the formation of mountains.

2. Why do people who are used to living at or near sea level have difficulty at higher altitudes?

CRITICAL THINKING

3. Compare and contrast folded mountains and fault-block mountains.

4. Suppose a Sherpa moved to a lower altitude. How might his or her blood cells adapt to conditions at the lower altitude?

REFLECT & EVALUATE

Word Power

Write the letter of the term that best completes each sentence. *Not all terms will be used*.

1. The solid, rocky layer of Earth about 100 km thick is the ___.
2. When a fluid has a hot surface below and a cold surface above, this condition produces ___.
3. Pikes Peak is a ___.
4. Tectonic plates interact at ___.
5. Tectonic plates move apart at ___.

a. asthenosphere
b. convection
c. divergent boundaries
d. dome mountain
e. folded mountains
f. lithosphere
g. plate boundaries

Check What You Know

Write the word in each pair that correctly completes each sentence.

1. Volcanoes form when (magma, lava) erupts onto Earth's surface.
2. Pikes Peak in Colorado is an example of a (dome, folded) mountain.
3. The (lower, higher) air pressure at higher altitudes means that less oxygen is taken in with each breath.
4. The hot rock in the asthenosphere rises to the lithosphere because it is (less, more) dense than the surrounding materials.

Problem Solving

1. You are in a research vehicle riding along a convection current in Earth's upper mantle. Describe the journey.

2. You skid on a small rug into a wall. How is what happens to the rug like tectonic plates building mountains?

3. The San Andreas Fault in California is a transform-fault boundary between the North American Plate and the Pacific Plate. Describe and model how the plates are moving along this boundary.

BUILD YOUR PORTFOLIO

Look at the map. Describe what features you might see along the convergent boundary.

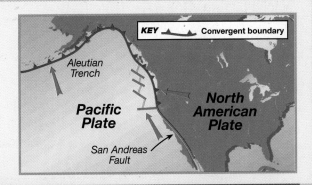

CHAPTER 3

SHAKE, RATTLE, AND ROLL

Many men and women in science try to solve problems that affect people's daily lives. Earthquakes have terrified people throughout history, and they continue to threaten loss of life and property today. How can science help?

PEOPLE USING SCIENCE

Seismologist Among the first people to investigate an earthquake are seismologists (sīz mäl′ə jists). These scientists study how and why earthquakes happen. Waverly Person is the chief of the National Earthquake Information Service in Denver, Colorado. He and his staff monitor movements in Earth's crust, using seismographs and other technology.

Seismologists examine the strength of each earthquake, how long it lasts, and where it is located. They exchange ideas about why an earthquake has happened. Over the years, seismologists have developed hypotheses about where future earthquakes will happen. How might such predictions be useful?

Coming Up

Waverly Person checking a seismograph

WHAT CAUSES EARTHQUAKES, AND HOW CAN THEY BE COMPARED?

Picture two railroad cars rolling past each other on side-by-side tracks. Could they get by each other if their sides were touching? Some tectonic plates are a little like these trains. This investigation is about the sudden changes that can occur when plates that touch move past one another.

Activity

A Model of Sliding Plates

Did you ever try to slide a heavy box over a rough sidewalk and have the box get stuck? Tectonic plates have rough surfaces, too. What happens when the plates keep pushing but the rocks don't slide?

- -

Procedure

1. Cover two blocks of wood with coarse sandpaper. Use rubber bands, as shown, to hold the sandpaper on the blocks of wood.

2. **Predict** what will happen if you hold the sandpaper surfaces tightly against each other and then try to slide the blocks past each other. **Record** your prediction in your *Science Notebook*.

Step 1

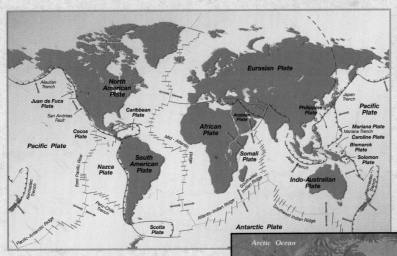

▲ Tectonic-plates map. For a larger map, see pages B20 and B21.

3. Try sliding the blocks past each other. (Hold together the surfaces on which there are no rubber bands.) **Observe** what happens and **record** your observations.

4. Explain how this action might be like two tectonic plates passing each other.

5. Now list the places shown on your tectonic-plates map where plates are sliding past each other. For example, note that the Pacific Plate and the North American Plate are sliding past each other near the west coast of the United States.

6. Find the same places on the Earth-features map. List any features you find in those places that seem to be related to the motion of the plates.

Analyze and Conclude

1. Think about places you identified in steps 5 and 6. Have you read or heard anything about any of these locations that might involve changes in Earth's crust? What do you conclude might happen when two tectonic plates slide past each other?

2. Did you find anything that looks as if it might be caused by the sliding of two plates? If so, what did you find?

▲ Earth-features map. For a larger map, see page B41.

INVESTIGATE FURTHER!

EXPERIMENT

Find two bricks. Slide one over the other. Do they slide easily? What do you hear? What do you feel? What happens when two smooth rock surfaces slide past each other?

B53

Sliding Plates

Reading Focus What are earthquakes, and where are they most likely to occur?

VOL. LV...NO. 17,617. • • • • •   NEW YORK, THURS

OVER 500 DEAD, $200,000,000 LOST IN SAN FRANCISCO EARTHQUAKE

Nearly Half the City Is in Ruins and 50,000 Are Homeless.

firemen and United States soldiers, who assisted them, blew down building af ter building. Their efforts, however were useless, so far as checking the headway of the flames was concerned

The shortage of water was due t the breaking of the mains of the Sprin Valley Water Company at San Mateo The water needed so badly in the cit; rad in a flood over San Mateo.

Burning of the Opera House.

▲ City Hall after the 1906 San Francisco earthquake; a 1906 newspaper headline

It was a few minutes after 5:00 A.M. on April 18, 1906. Many San Franciscans were awakened by a deep rumbling of the ground beneath them. Homes, stores, offices, hotels, churches, and bridges collapsed. Sergeant Jesse Cook, a police officer, observed, "The whole street was undulating [waving]. It was as if the waves of the ocean were coming toward me."

The "Big One" of 1906

Scientists estimate that the earthquake that struck San Francisco in 1906 would have had a reading of about 8.3 on the Richter scale. (You'll read more about the Richter scale in "Our Active Earth" on pages B56 and B57.) The earthquake

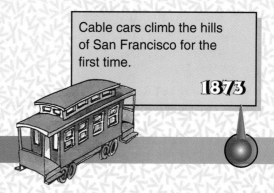

Cable cars climb the hills of San Francisco for the first time.

1873

1848
Gold is discovered at Sutter's Mill.

lasted for only a little over a minute. But its effects were enormous. About 500 people died, and nearly 250,000 were left homeless. Water mains were destroyed. Fires due to broken gas lines raged throughout the city for days. More than 28,000 buildings were destroyed by the fires.

Shortly after the earthquake, San Franciscans began to rebuild their destroyed city and their disrupted lives. By December 1906 many new buildings stood where others had collapsed. Within about three years, 20,000 buildings had been constructed to replace those lost to fire and to the quake itself.

Today, just as in 1906, people ask "What are earthquakes? Why do these tremors happen in some places and not in others?" An earthquake is a vibration of Earth, caused by a sudden release of energy stored along a fault. Most earthquakes occur along tectonic plate boundaries, places on Earth where vast slabs of rock separate, collide, or slide past one another.

Faults

The 1906 earthquake occurred when blocks of rock deep within Earth's surface began to move along a crack called the San Andreas Fault. A fault is a large crack in layers of rock along which movement has occurred. The San Andreas Fault runs through much of California and separates the North American Plate from the Pacific Plate. The 1906 San Francisco earthquake wasn't the first "earthshaking" event to occur along the San Andreas Fault, and it wasn't the last. Many large earthquakes have struck that region since 1906. A major earthquake struck the San Francisco Bay area in October 1989. That quake, measuring 7.1 on the Richter scale, caused 63 deaths and $7 billion in damage. Scientists predict that a much larger earthquake—the "Big One"—is yet to come. ■

Internet Field Trip

Visit **www.eduplace.com** to learn more about plate movement along the San Andreas Fault.

San Francisco is struck by an earthquake estimated to have had a reading of 8.3 on the Richter scale.

1906

An earthquake measuring 7.1 on the Richter scale strikes San Francisco.

1989

1901
The vacuum cleaner is invented.

1995
More than 5,000 people die in an earthquake that strikes Kobe, Japan.

Our Active Earth

Reading Focus How do scientists measure the strength of an earthquake, and how can they predict future earthquakes?

Earth is an ever-changing planet. Some changes happen in a matter of seconds. Other changes occur over months or years. Soils are eroded by water, wind, and gravity. Mountains take hundreds, thousands, or even millions of years to form and just as long to be worn away. And some changes, such as those caused by earthquakes, occur suddenly and violently.

Earthquakes

Earthquakes usually last for only a few minutes. But it takes many years to build up the energy that is released during an earthquake. As blocks of rocks move past one another along faults, friction prevents some sections of rock from slipping very much. Instead, the rocks bend and change shape, until the force becomes too great. It is only when the rocks suddenly slide past each other that an earthquake occurs.

An **earthquake** is a vibration of Earth, caused by the release of energy that has been stored along a fault. Most earthquakes occur along tectonic plate boundaries. California is one area where earthquakes are likely to occur. Part of southern California is on the edge of the Pacific Plate, which is moving slowly toward the northwest.

The San Andreas Fault

During the 30-million-year history of the San Andreas Fault in California, hundreds of earthquakes and many thousands of aftershocks have occurred along its length of 1,200 km (720 mi). An **aftershock** is a shock that occurs after the principal shock of an earthquake.

In October 1989 an earthquake centered in Loma Prieta, California, was felt as far away as Oregon and Nevada. This earthquake caused more than 60 deaths and registered 7.1 on the Richter scale.

The Richter Scale

If you've ever listened to or read a news report about an earthquake, you've heard the term *Richter scale*. The **Richter scale**, with numbers ranging from 1 to 10, describes the magnitude,

Damage caused by the Loma Prieta, California, earthquake in October 1989 ▼

or strength, of an earthquake. The **magnitude** of an earthquake is the amount of energy released by the quake. The Richter scale is named after the American seismologist Charles Richter. Minor earthquakes have magnitudes of 4 or less. The largest recorded earthquakes have magnitudes of about 8.5.

Each increase of 1.0 on the Richter scale represents a difference of about 30 times more energy than the previous number. For example, an earthquake measuring 5.0 on the Richter scale releases about 30 times more energy

than a quake measuring 4.0. Likewise, an earthquake measuring 5.7 on the Richter scale releases about 30 times less energy than an earthquake measuring 6.7 on the scale.

| Major Earthquakes of the San Andreas Fault ||
Richter Scale Magnitude	Earthquake
8.25	San Francisco April 18, 1906
8.25	Fort Tejon Jan. 9, 1857
7.4	Yucca Valley June 28, 1992
7.1	Imperial Valley May 9, 1940
7.1	Loma Prieta Oct. 17–18, 1989
6.6	Superstition Hills Nov. 24, 1987
6.5	Coalinga May 2, 1983

Using Math *The Pacific and the North American plates border the San Andreas Fault. About how many times more energy was released during the 1992 Yucca Valley earthquake than in the 1983 Coalinga earthquake?*

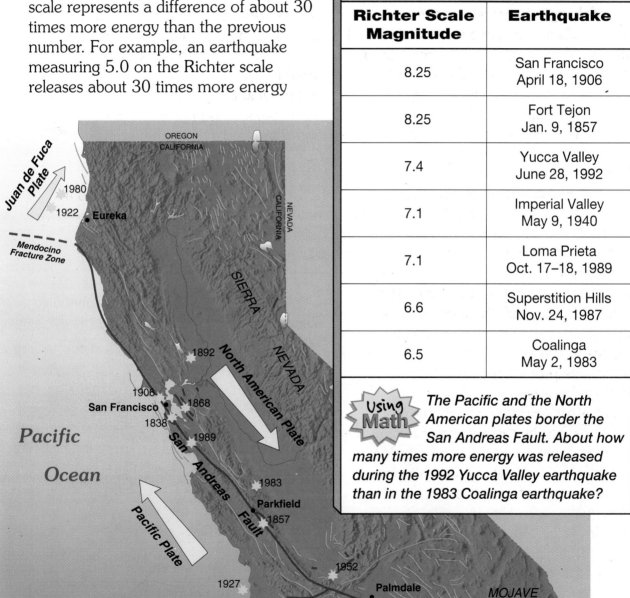

Now study the table and map on page B57, showing some of the earthquakes that occurred along the San Andreas Fault over the past century. Where along the San Andreas did most of the quakes occur? Where did the strongest earthquakes occur? Then look at the map below. Where is the strongest earthquake likely to occur in the future?

Predicting Earthquakes

Scientists know that earthquakes are more common in some parts of the world than in others. Yet the actual timing of these Earth movements is difficult to predict. Seismologists, scientists who study earthquakes, have no sure way of knowing when or where an earthquake will strike or how strong it will be. They can only give estimates of the probability that an earthquake will strike in a certain place within a certain span of years.

Once in a while, seismologists are lucky in predicting earthquakes. In 1988, seismologists with the United States Geological Survey predicted that Loma Prieta, California, was likely to have an earthquake. Loma Prieta is along the San Andreas Fault. On October 17, 1989, a severe earthquake struck Loma Prieta and nearby San Francisco and Oakland.

Seismologists have found that there are changes in Earth that come before most earthquakes. Knowing this, the seismologists closely watch instruments that measure and record these changes. Seismologists are especially careful to watch the instruments in regions where

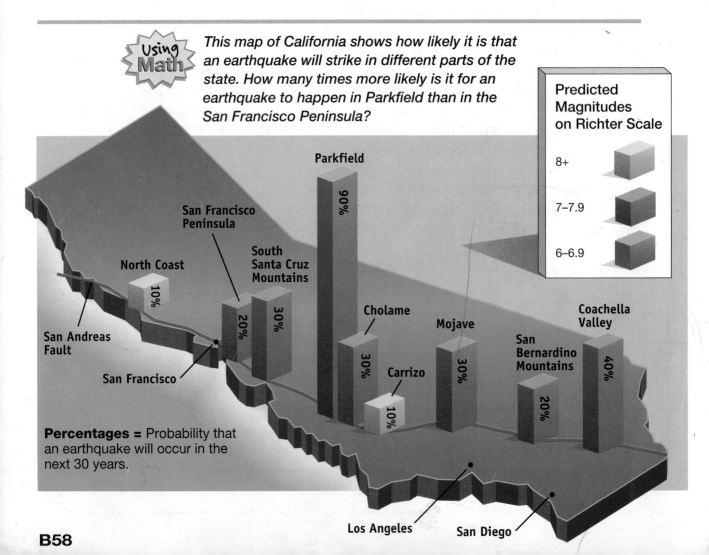

Using Math This map of California shows how likely it is that an earthquake will strike in different parts of the state. How many times more likely is it for an earthquake to happen in Parkfield than in the San Francisco Peninsula?

Predicted Magnitudes on Richter Scale

8+

7–7.9

6–6.9

Parkfield 90%

San Francisco Peninsula 20%

South Santa Cruz Mountains 30%

North Coast 10%

Cholame 30%

Mojave 30%

Coachella Valley 40%

San Bernardino Mountains 20%

Carrizo 10%

San Andreas Fault

San Francisco

Percentages = Probability that an earthquake will occur in the next 30 years.

Los Angeles   San Diego

earthquakes are likely to occur. For example, changes in the tilt of slabs of rock below ground can indicate that an earthquake is brewing. Studies have shown that rock formations will swell before an earthquake. Changes in Earth's magnetic and gravitational fields can mean an earthquake is soon to strike. Increases in the amount of a radioactive gas called radon from within Earth often come before an earthquake. Micro-earthquakes, or minor tremors, can also indicate that a more intense earthquake will strike an area.

Just how accurate are these warnings? Some scientists argue that watching changes in various instruments can lead to the prediction of earthquakes. Eleven days before the 1989 Loma Prieta earthquake, an instrument in the area recorded natural radio waves from Earth that were nearly 30 times stronger than usual. Just a few hours before the earthquake struck, these radio signals became so strong that they shot off the scale of the instrument.

A study by scientists at the Southern California Earthquake Center suggests that in the next 30 years there will be a severe earthquake in southern California. Exactly when and where it will strike is anyone's guess. ■

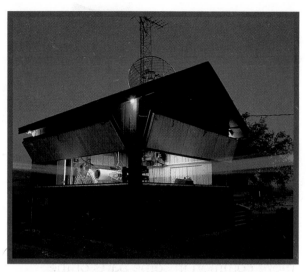

▲ **Laser beams are being used to monitor Earth's movements and to predict quakes.**

INVESTIGATE FURTHER!

RESEARCH

Some people believe that animals are very sensitive to the changes that occur before events such as storms and earthquakes. Find out about this hypothesis concerning animal behavior before an earthquake as a possible warning sign for people. What do you think about this idea?

INVESTIGATION 1 WRAP-UP

THINK IT
WRITE IT

REVIEW

1. How is the movement of tectonic plates related to the occurrence of earthquakes?

2. What is the Richter scale, and what does each increase of 1.0 represent?

CRITICAL THINKING

3. Is the likelihood of an earthquake greater in California or New York? Explain.

4. Should scientists alert the public about an increase in the strength of natural radio waves? Why or why not?

INVESTIGATION 2

WHAT HAPPENS TO EARTH'S CRUST DURING AN EARTHQUAKE?

Have you ever pushed a desk across a floor? Sometimes the desk starts to vibrate, and you can feel the vibrations in your hands and arms. In this investigation you'll find out how this experience is similar to what happens during an earthquake.

Activity

Shake It!

In this activity you'll make a model for observing what can happen to buildings during an earthquake. In your model you'll make the vibrations.

MATERIALS
- small block of wood
- clear plastic bowl, filled with sand
- water
- measuring cup
- clear plastic bowl, filled with gelatin
- *Science Notebook*

Procedure

1. Think of a block of wood as a building and a bowl filled with sand as the surface of Earth. Stand a block of wood in a bowl full of sand.

2. Predict what will happen if you shake the bowl. Record your prediction in your *Science Notebook*.

3. Shake the bowl rapidly by sliding it back and forth. Observe what happens to the block and the surface of the sand. Record your observations.

A highway toppled during the 1995 earthquake in Kobe, Japan. ▶

4. Pour water over the sand until the water is at the same level as the sand. Again stand the wooden block on the sand. **Predict** what will happen to the block if you shake the bowl with the wet sand. Repeat the shaking, **observe** what happens, and **record** your observations.

5. Now **predict** what will happen when you set the block in a bowl of gelatin and shake the bowl. Try it; then **record** your observations.

Analyze and Conclude

1. During the "earthquake," what happened to the dry sand? the wet sand? the gelatin? What, do you think, did the dry sand, the wet sand, and the gelatin represent?

2. What happened to the "building" as it stood on the different surfaces?

3. Which model showed the most damage to the "building"? What evidence supports your conclusions?

Step 4

UNIT PROJECT LINK

At 5:30 P.M. on March 27, 1964, the most powerful earthquake to hit North America struck Anchorage, Alaska. More than 130 people in Alaska and 12 people in Crescent City, California, were killed by the tsunami that followed the quake. (You'll find out about tsunamis on pages B74–75.)

Use a map to trace how far the tsunami traveled. Then compute the distance that the tsunami traveled. Look at an earthquake map of the world. Outline in red those North American coastlines that might experience tsunamis.

TechnologyLink
For more help with your Unit Project, go to **www.eduplace.com**.

Bend Till It Breaks

Reading Focus What are faults, and how do tectonic plates move along them?

Imagine that you are holding a flexible wooden stick that is about 2 cm wide and 1 m long. You are holding one end in each hand and are gently bending the stick. If you stop bending the stick, it will return to its original shape. What will happen if you keep on bending it? Eventually it will snap!

Forces and Faults

Although Earth's rocks are hard and brittle, in some ways they can behave like the bending wooden stick. You probably know that a force is a push or a pull. If a pulling force is applied slowly to rocks, they will stretch. But like the wooden stick, the rocks will break or snap if the

Movement Along Faults

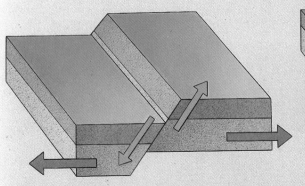

NORMAL FAULT The rock slabs are pulling apart, and one slab has moved up, while the other has moved down along the fault.

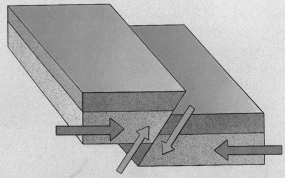

REVERSE FAULT The rock slabs are pushing together, and one rock slab has pushed under the other along the fault.

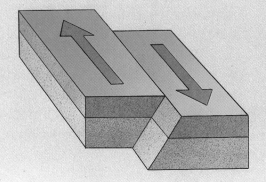

STRIKE-SLIP FAULT Slabs of rock are moving horizontally past each other along a fault. This type of fault is produced by twisting and tearing of layers of rock. The San Andreas Fault is an example of a strike-slip fault.

force on them is too great. A break in rocks along which the rocks have moved is called a **fault**.

What do you think happens when rocks are squeezed together from opposite sides? If pushing forces are applied to rocks, they bend, or fold. But, just as with pulling forces, pushing forces will eventually cause rocks to break. So, pushing forces also create faults in rocks. You can see the effect of these pushing forces in the drawing of the reverse fault on page B62.

Movement Along Faults

Forces may continue to be applied to slabs of rock that contain faults. The forces, which may be either up-and-down or sideways, may continue for many years. The three drawings on page B62 show examples of the main kinds of movement along faults. In time the forces on the rocks become so great that the slabs overcome the friction that has kept them from moving. Then the rock slabs move violently along the fault.

Earthquakes and Faults

Imagine that your hands are the two rock walls on either side of a fault. Picture rubbing your hands together when they are in soapy water. Then picture rubbing them together when they are dry. Sometimes the movement of rocks along a fault is quick and smooth, like the rubbing together of soap-covered hands. But at other times the movement can be slow and rough. As the movement causes rocks to lock and bend, energy builds up in the rocks, much as energy builds up in a flexed wooden stick. When the energy in the rocks is released, an earthquake occurs.

You know that an earthquake is a vibration of the Earth produced by the quick release of this stored energy. The point at which an earthquake begins is the **focus** of the earthquake. Most earthquakes begin below the surface. The point on Earth's surface directly above the focus is called the **epicenter** (ep'i sent ər) of the earthquake.

Earthquakes can begin anywhere from about 5 km (3 mi) to 700 km (420 mi) below Earth's surface. Scientists have found that most earthquakes are shallow—they occur within 60 km (about 35 mi) of the surface. The most destructive earthquakes seem to be the shallow ones. The focus of the 1906 San Francisco earthquake was no deeper than about 15 km (9 mi).

Earthquake Focus and Epicenter

Waves are sent out in all directions from the focus of the earthquake. Notice that the epicenter is the spot on the surface of Earth that lies directly above the focus. ▼

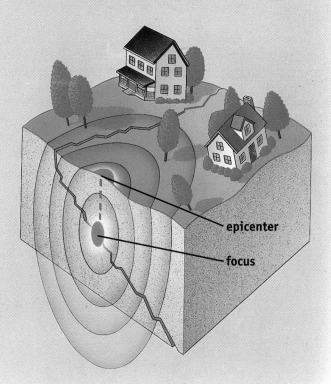

epicenter

focus

Earthquakes Around the World

When earthquake locations are plotted on a world map, patterns emerge. From the map on page B17, you can see that earthquakes occur along certain belts, or zones. Do these zones look familiar? They should! Most earthquakes occur along tectonic plate boundaries. Many occur near the edges of the Pacific Ocean.

Japan, the western United States, Chile, and parts of Central America are just a few of the areas around the edges of the Pacific Ocean that experience earthquakes.

Where do most earthquakes occur in the United States? Even without looking at a map, you probably could have guessed that most earthquakes in the United States happen in California. Now look closely at the map on page B17. Some earthquakes have occurred in the eastern part of the country—far from the San Andreas Fault. Is your area at risk for an earthquake? Although most earthquakes in the United States occur in California, earthquakes can happen anywhere in this country. What is the risk that your state or surrounding states will experience an earthquake?

Earthquake Waves

Have you ever stood in a pool, lake, or ocean and felt water waves break against your body? Have you ever "done the wave" at a sports event? What do all waves have in common? A wave is a rhythmic disturbance that carries energy. The energy released by an earthquake

Science in Literature

A Rude Awakening

"The moment I felt the house tremble and the plaster and bric-a-brac begin to fall, I leaped out of bed and rushed out to the front door, which I had a time unbolting on account of shifting of the house, and while trying to get it opened I was bumped back and forth against it until I was sure the house would fall...."

Each chapter begins with a quotation from a letter written by Edith Irvine—a photographer who experienced the 1906 earthquake. Read about the impact of the earthquake on people's everyday lives, view photographs, and read more of Irvine's letter in *Earthquake at Dawn* by Kristiana Gregory.

Earthquake at Dawn
by Kristiana Gregory
Harcourt Brace, 1992

travels outward from the earth-quake's focus in all directions. The energy is carried by waves. Much of what is known about Earth's structure has been learned from studying the effects of earthquake waves.

There are three different kinds of earthquake waves: P waves, S waves, and L waves. The drawings and captions below show how the three kinds of waves differ. ■

Earthquakes can severely damage property. ▶

P WAVES P waves, or primary waves, move out in all directions from the earthquake focus. These waves push and pull the rocks, causing them to vibrate in the same direction in which the wave is traveling.

S WAVES S waves, or secondary waves, move out in all directions from the earthquake focus. These waves cause the rocks to move at right angles to the direction in which the wave is traveling.

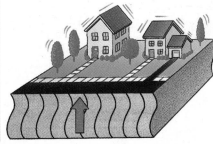

L WAVES L waves, or surface waves, are caused by P and S waves. L waves move along the surface, causing rock material to move up and down. These are the most destructive earthquake waves.

INVESTIGATION 2 WRAP-UP

REVIEW

1. Describe the changes taking place in Earth's crust during an earthquake. What forces cause these changes?

2. Explain the difference between the focus and the epicenter of an earthquake.

CRITICAL THINKING

3. What is the connection between a fault and the production of an earthquake?

4. Why, do you think, are L waves the most destructive of the three types of waves?

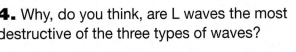

HOW ARE EARTHQUAKES LOCATED AND MEASURED?

The newscaster read, "The earthquake last night in Prince William Sound, Alaska, measured 8.4 on the Richter scale. It was a BIG one!" What tools and methods do scientists use to measure how strong an earthquake is or determine where it began?

Activity

Shake It Harder!

The energy of an earthquake is measured with a device called a seismograph. In this activity you'll build a working model of a seismograph and then test how it works as you create your own small "earthquake."

Procedure

1. Tightly wrap several lengths of string around the seat of a chair in two places (about 10 cm apart), as shown on page B67.

> See **SCIENCE** *and* **MATH TOOLBOX** page H6 if you need to review *Using a Tape Measure or Ruler.*

2. Tightly wrap string around two heavy books in two places (about 6 cm from each end of the books).

3. Tape a fine-point marker to one end of the books. The tip of the marker should hang about 3–4 cm below the edges of the books.

MATERIALS

- string
- chair
- metric ruler
- 2 heavy books
- masking tape
- fine-point marker
- table
- shelf paper (2 m long)
- *Science Notebook*

SAFETY

Be careful not to push or shake the chair off the tabletop while doing this activity.

4. Place a length of shelf paper on the top of a table. Place the chair with the string wrapped around the seat on the table, above the shelf paper. Make sure the legs of the chair don't touch the shelf paper.

5. Using string, suspend the books from the chair so that the tip of the marker just touches the surface of the shelf paper. Make sure that the books are parallel to the paper.

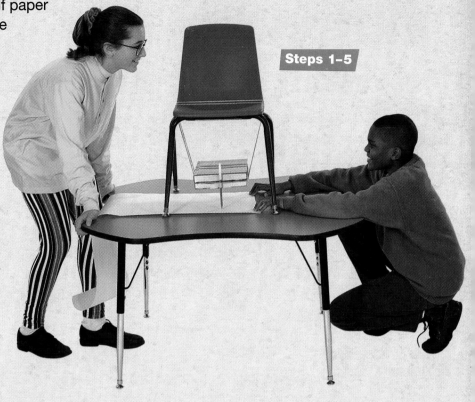

Steps 1–5

6. You have just built a model seismograph. You'll use it to measure an "earthquake" that you'll create by gently shaking the table from side to side. The shelf paper will become the seismogram, or record of the earthquake.

7. Predict what will be shown on the seismogram if you shake the table gently. Record your predictions in your *Science Notebook*.

8. Place your hands against the side of the table and gently shake it as another member of your group slowly pulls the paper under the pen.

9. Repeat step 8. This time, shake the table a little harder (move the table farther but not faster).

Analyze and Conclude

1. How did your prediction in step 7 compare with what actually happened?

2. How did changing the energy with which you shook the table change the seismogram? How did the record on the seismogram for the first "earthquake" differ from that for the second "earthquake"?

3. How do you think a real seismograph is like the one you built? How might it be different?

INVESTIGATE FURTHER!

EXPERIMENT

Does the seismograph work as well if you shake the table in the same direction in which the paper is being pulled? What would this mean with a real seismograph?
Is there any connection between the length of the strings and the working of the seismograph?

Activity

Locating Earthquakes

The point on Earth's surface above the origin of an earthquake is called the epicenter. The location of the epicenter can be found by comparing the travel times of P waves and S waves at different locations.

MATERIALS

- metric ruler
- Earthquake Travel Time graph
- map of the United States
- drawing compass
- *Science Notebook*

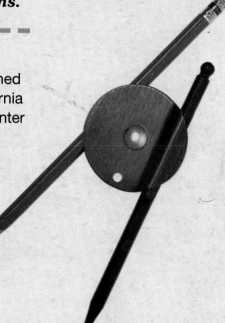

- -

Data

The table below shows the times at which shock waves reached three cities in the United States after the earthquake in California on October 17–18, 1989. Use this information to find the epicenter of that earthquake.

Procedure

1. In your *Science Notebook*, copy the table below. For each city, **calculate** the difference in arrival time between the P wave and the S wave. **Record** your results.

Math Hint *When you subtract, remember to rename 1 minute as 60 seconds.*

Arrival Times of P Waves and S Waves (hr: min: sec)			
City	P Wave	S Wave	Difference
Tucson, AZ	5:06:35	5:08:50	
Billings, MT	5:07:10	5:10:00	
Houston, TX	5:09:10	5:13:35	

2. Place a sheet of paper along the *y*-axis of the Earthquake Travel Time graph provided by your teacher. On the sheet of paper, mark the time interval between the arrival of the P wave and the S wave in Tucson. For example, if the time difference is 4 minutes, you would make marks next to "0" and "4."

3. Keep the edge of the paper parallel to the y-axis. Move the paper to the right and up until the space between the marks matches the space between the S-wave curve and the P-wave curve.

4. The point on the x-axis directly below (or along) the edge of the paper is the distance from Tucson to the epicenter of the quake. **Record** this distance.

5. Repeat steps 2 through 4 for Billings and Houston.

6. On a United States map, use a drawing compass to draw a circle around each city in the chart. Use the calculated distance from the quake as the radius of each circle. The point at which the circles intersect is the epi-center of the October 1989 earthquake.

Step 6

Analyze and Conclude

1. What is the distance from each of the cities to the epicenter?

2. Where was the epicenter of the October 1989 earthquake?

3. What are the fewest reporting locations necessary to locate an epicenter? Explain your answer.

4. **Compare** your results with those of other members of your class. Account for any differences you find.

INVESTIGATE FURTHER!

TAKE ACTION

Contact or visit an office of the U.S. Geological Survey for more information about locating earthquakes. You may write to the U.S. Geological Survey at Distribution Branch, Box 25286, Federal Center, Denver, CO 80225.

Activity

Be an Architect

The competition is stiff! You and your teammates will build an "earthquake-proof" building. Then you will create a mini-earthquake and test your building. Will it remain standing? Which team will have the most earthquake-proof building?

MATERIALS

- several small cardboard boxes
- masking tape
- large aluminum pan
- clay
- sand
- soil
- wooden dowels
- timer with a second hand
- *Science Notebook*

Procedure

1. With other members of your team, **design** a high-rise "building" that will not tip over in an earthquake. The building must be made of cardboard boxes and any other materials, such as clay, sand, soil, and wooden dowels, that your teacher provides for you. You will subject this building to an "earthquake" that you create by shaking your desk or table. **Draw** your design in your *Science Notebook*.

2. With the rest of your class, **design** a standard that describes when a building is considered earthquake-proof. Make sure the standard will clearly separate good designs from poor designs following an earthquake.

3. **Construct** your building on top of your desk or table.

4. **Predict** how well your building will withstand an earthquake. **Discuss** your prediction with other members of your group.

Step 1

5. With the rest of your class, determine how long the earthquake will last and how strongly you'll shake the table. Note the length of time the building remains standing during the earthquake. Note whether the building undergoes any kind of damage during the earthquake. Use the standard to determine if your building is earthquake-proof. **Record** all observations.

6. **Compare** your results with those of other groups of students in your class.

Analyze and Conclude

1. How closely did your results agree with your prediction of how well your building could withstand an earthquake?

2. How did your design compare with those of other teams of students?

3. Which design best stood up to the earthquake? What was important about that design?

Technology Link CD-ROM

INVESTIGATE FURTHER!

Use the **Science Processor CD-ROM**, *The Changing Earth* (Investigation 3, Feel the Quake!) to learn about S waves, P waves, and seismographs. Then find the epicenter of an earthquake.

The Seismograph

Reading Focus What does a seismograph do, and how does it work?

Energy from an earthquake travels outward from its focus in all directions, in much the same way that energy is released when a pebble is dropped into a pond. Seismic waves travel at different speeds through Earth's crust and upper mantle. P waves are the fastest; L waves are the slowest. These waves are recorded by an instrument called a **seismograph** (sīz′mə graf).

One of the earliest seismographs used bronze balls to detect earthquake waves. The dragons on this Chinese earthquake detector clenched the bronze balls in their mouths. When the ground vibrated, one or more balls fell from the dragons' mouths. The balls landed in the mouths of waiting metal toads around the base of the instrument. The noise the balls made when they reached the toads' mouths alerted people to the fact that the ground had shaken. People could then determine the direction from which the waves came by observing the direction in which the dragons' empty mouths pointed.

A modern seismograph is a device that generally includes a frame (mounted to bedrock), a weight, a pen, and a rotating drum. In the activity on pages B66 and B67, most of these parts are included in the model seismograph.

A pendulum seismograph consists of a support frame, a heavy weight to which a pen is attached, and a rotating drum. This type of seismograph measures side-to-side Earth movements. A spring seismograph measures up-and-down Earth movements. The drawings on page B73 show all the parts of these earthquake-recording devices.

This Chinese earthquake detector is known as Chang Heng's seismoscope. Chang Heng invented this seismoscope in A.D. 132. How many years ago was that?

Parts of the Seismograph

Spring Seismograph

Pendulum Seismograph

1 SUPPORT FRAME
The frame is anchored to solid rock, deep beneath the soil.

2 WEIGHT
The weight of a seismograph keeps the pen steady.

3 MAGNET
The magnet reduces the motion of the weight.

4 WIRE OR SPRING
In the spring seismograph, the spring supports the weight. In the pendulum seismograph, the wire keeps the weight suspended above the rotating drum.

5 PEN
The pen, which touches the rotating drum, records movements caused by seismic waves.

6 ROTATING DRUM
The drum rotates, or turns, all the time. When seismic movements of Earth occur, the pen touching the drum records these movements.

INVESTIGATE FURTHER!

RESEARCH

Find out about early seismographs. How are they like modern ones? How are they different from modern ones?

Earthquakes on the Sea Floor

Reading Focus What happens when an earthquake occurs on the ocean floor?

Tsunamis—What Are They?

You have probably heard the term *tsunami* (tso͞o nä′mē). This Japanese word means "harbor wave." You may have heard such waves incorrectly called tidal waves. A **tsunami** has nothing to do with ocean tides. Rather, this seismic sea wave forms when an earthquake occurs on the ocean floor. The earthquake's energy causes the sea floor to move up and down. This movement can produce destructive waves of water. Why are these waves so dangerous?

Most tsunamis are related to the earthquakes that occur around the edges of the Pacific Plate. In these areas, massive slabs of rock are being forced down into the mantle. Plates often lock when they collide, allowing energy to build up. Eventually this energy is released as

1 TSUNAMI FORMING
When an earthquake triggers a tsunami in deep water, the wave's height is only about a meter (3 ft).

2 TSUNAMI TRAVELING
In the open ocean, the distance between two crests or troughs can be about 100 km (60 mi). A tsunami is often unnoticed in the open ocean, even though it can be traveling close to 800 km/h (500 mph)!

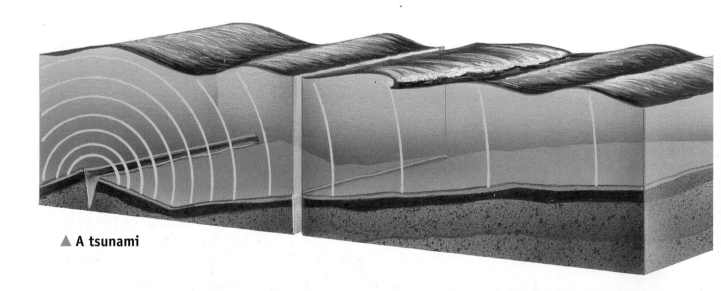

▲ A tsunami

an earthquake, which raises and lowers the nearby ocean floor. This movement sets a tsunami in motion.

Destructive Walls of Water

Most tsunamis are caused by earthquakes. But landslides on the ocean floor and volcanic eruptions can also cause tsunamis. Fortunately, tsunamis only occur about once a year. Study the table on page B76. What was the cause of the 1993 tsunami that began off the coast of Japan?

As with earthquakes, tsunamis cause destruction where they begin as well as along their paths. The tsunami that began with the 1964 Alaskan earthquake, for example, struck the Alaskan coastline and then Vancouver Island in Canada. Waves also struck California

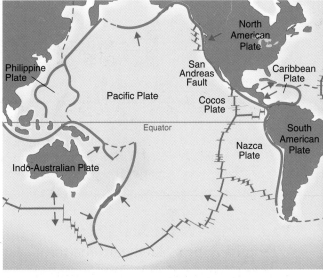

▲ **Tsunamis are common along the shores close to the edges of the Pacific Plate.**

and the Hawaiian Islands. The seismic sea waves finally lost their energy at the Japanese coast—over 6,400 km (about 4,000 mi) from their point of origin!

---

3 TSUNAMI NEARING SHORE
As the wave makes its way toward shore, it slows down because of friction between the advancing water and the ocean floor. But as the water becomes shallower, the height of the wave increases.

4 TSUNAMI STRIKING SHORE
Close to shore a tsunami can reach a height of tens of meters! On March 2, 1933, a tsunami that struck the Japanese island of Honshu reached a height of 14 m (46 ft).

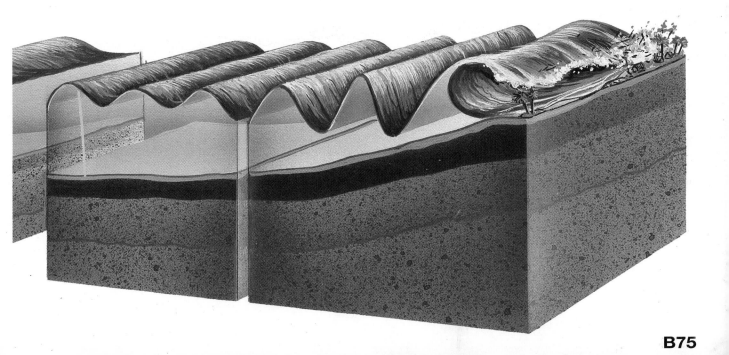

Selected Tsunamis and Their Effects

Year	Place of Origin	Cause	Height of Water (m)	Deaths
1883	East Indies	volcano	>40 m	>36,000
1896	Japan	earthquake	38 m	26,000
1946	Alaska	earthquake	>30 m	164
1960	Chile	earthquake	6 m	144
1992	Indonesia	earthquake	10 m	71,000
1993	Japan	earthquake	32 m	120

Predicting Tsunamis

Unlike earthquakes and volcanic eruptions, some tsunamis can be predicted. In 1946 the Tsunami Warning System was established to forewarn people in the areas surrounding the Pacific Ocean of these destructive events.

There are two tsunami warning centers in the United States. One center is near Honolulu, Hawaii; the other is just north of Anchorage, in Palmer, Alaska. Scientists at these centers use satellites to gather seismic data from more than 20 countries that border the Pacific Ocean. If earthquakes registering more than about 6.5 on the Richter scale are found, warnings are sent to other centers.

Recall that in the open ocean, tsunamis are hardly detectable at the surface of the water. So in addition to setting up warning centers, scientists with the National Oceanic and Atmospheric Administration are studying the usefulness of tsunami sensors that rest on the ocean floor. These devices look promising. In water 4,000 to 5,000 m (13,200 to 16,500 ft) deep, the sensors can detect a change in sea level of less than a millimeter!

Tsunami sensors are flexible metal tubes that are weighted down on the ocean floor. Each tube measures the mass of the water column above it. When a wave passes over the tube, the mass of the water column increases, causing the tube to straighten. After the wave has passed, the tube coils up again. The straightening and coiling of the tubes record changes in water pressure—and the presence of large waves. Such changes can show the presence of tsunamis. ■

Huge waves from a tsunami strike the shore. ▶

Designing for Survival

Reading Focus How are buildings constructed to withstand the force of an earthquake?

SCIENCE
TECHNOLOGY
& SOCIETY

Much of the damage done during an earthquake is caused by the earthquake's L waves. Recall that as L waves move, they cause surface rocks to move up and down. These destructive waves cause the foundations of most buildings to move with the passing waves. The buildings themselves, however, tend to resist the movements.

Because of the damage earthquakes can do, building codes in the western United States and in other earthquake-prone areas of the world have been

CONVENTIONAL FOUNDATION With this foundation, the ground movement is exaggerated on upper floors. The building "drifts," and a lot of damage occurs. Upper floors can collapse onto lower floors.

EARTHQUAKE-RESISTANT FOUNDATION This foundation is built of steel and rubber around concrete columns with lead cores. Since the frame is flexible, the floors can move from side to side, and the building isn't badly damaged.

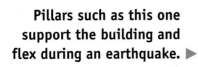

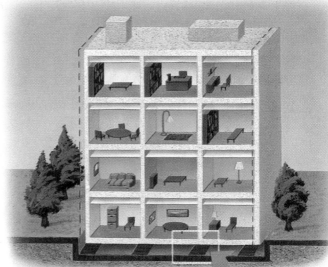

Pillars such as this one support the building and flex during an earthquake. ▶

changed. The new codes deal with the design of new buildings that will help to withstand earthquakes. The building codes also suggest ways to prevent damage in older buildings. Drawings in this resource show some ways that structures are strengthened against earthquakes. ■

Damage to the Golden Gate Freeway following an earthquake in California in 1989 ▼

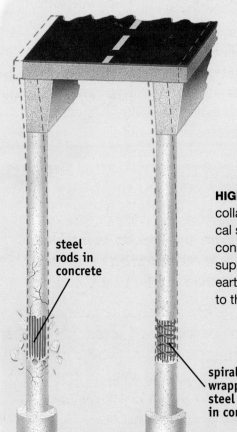

steel
rods in
concrete

spiral-
wrapped
steel rods
in concrete

HIGHWAY SUPPORT The column at the left will probably collapse in an earthquake. The column at the right has vertical steel rods that are spiral-wrapped in steel. This kind of construction could prevent collapse during a quake. Blocks supporting the columns should be able to move with the earthquake. At the same time, they must be firmly anchored to the columns.

━━━━━━━━━ **INVESTIGATION 3 WRAP-UP** ━━━━━━━━━

REVIEW

1. How does a seismograph measure an earthquake?

2. Explain how to locate the epicenter of an earthquake.

CRITICAL THINKING

3. Compare the effects of an earthquake in which the focus is under the ocean with an earthquake in which the focus is under land.

4. Why is it easier to design warning systems for tsunamis than it is for earthquakes?

REFLECT & EVALUATE

Word Power

Write the letter of the term that best completes each sentence. *Not all terms will be used*.

a. aftershock
b. earthquake
c. epicenter
d. fault
e. focus
f. Richter scale
g. seismograph

1. A vibration of Earth caused by a sudden release of energy stored in the crust is a (an) ——.
2. The main shock of an earthquake may be followed by a (an) ——.
3. The point at which an earthquake begins is the ——.
4. Rocks move along a break called a ——.
5. Earthquake waves are recorded by a (an) ——.

Check What You Know

Write the word in each pair that correctly completes each sentence.

1. The most destructive seismic waves are (L waves, S waves).
2. The strength of an earthquake is called its (epicenter, magnitude).
3. In a (reverse, normal) fault, the rock slabs push together.
4. Most tsunamis are caused by (earthquakes, volcanoes) on the ocean floor.
5. The Richter scale measures the (epicenter, magnitude) of an earthquake.

Problem Solving

1. Why are earthquakes in the United States more common on the West Coast than on the East Coast?
2. The 1993 earthquake near Los Angeles registered about 7.5 on the Richter scale. The 1964 earthquake near Anchorage, Alaska, registered 8.4. Compare the energy released in the two earthquakes.
3. Assume that you live in an area that experiences strong earthquakes. What could you do to prepare for an earthquake?

PORTFOLIO

What is shown in the drawing? Describe what might occur at such a location.

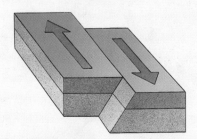

CHAPTER 4

VOLCANOES

Never trust a volcano! Millions of people live near active volcanoes. And over the past 20 years, sudden volcanic eruptions have killed over 28,000 people. Volcanoes have always been unpredictable and dangerous.

PEOPLE USING SCIENCE

Geophysicist The West Antarctic ice sheet stretches for hundreds of kilometers across the continent of Antarctica. This seemingly unchanging land with its thick cover of ice holds a secret that reminds us of how highly active Earth is.

Donald Blankenship and Robin Bell are both geophysicists (jē ō fiz'i sists), scientists who deal with Earth's weather, wind, earthquakes, and so forth. Blankenship and Bell were flying over the West Antarctic ice sheet when they noticed a caved-in area that measured 48 m deep and 6.4 km across. What could cause such a strange hole in the thick ice?

Using radar to see through the ice, the researchers discovered a 630-m mountain—a volcano. Imagine finding a volcano under a thick sheet of ice!

Coming Up

◀ Map showing presence of volcanic rock under the ice sheet

WHERE DO VOLCANOES OCCUR, AND HOW ARE THEY CLASSIFIED?

Volcanoes form when magma erupts from an opening in Earth's surface. Where are most volcanoes found in relation to tectonic plates? In this investigation you'll locate volcanoes and find out how they are compared and classified.

Activity

Worldwide Eruptions

You can plot volcanic eruptions from news articles to figure out how the eruptions relate to tectonic plates.

Step 3

Procedure

1. Break up into teams of researchers. Each team will research the location of active volcanoes during a different six-month period in the last two years. Collect news articles about active volcanoes throughout the world.

2. In your *Science Notebook,* record the date of each eruption, the name of the volcano, and its location. Also list whether each volcano is on a spreading ridge, on a plate margin near a descending plate, on a transform fault, or in the middle of a plate. Record how each volcano erupted: Was it a quiet lava flow, did it explode, or did it belch heavy clouds of ash?

See **SCIENCE** *and* **MATH TOOLBOX** page H11 if you need to review *Making a Chart to Organize Data.*

Selected Major Volcanic Eruptions			
Date	Volcano	Area	Death Toll
79	Vesuvius	Pompeii, Italy	3,000
1169	Etna	Sicily, Italy	15,000
1669	Etna	Sicily, Italy	20,000
1793	Unzen	Japan	50,000
1883	Krakatau	Java, Indonesia	36,000
1902	Pelée	St. Pierre, Martinique	28,000
1919	Kelut	Java, Indonesia	5,500
1980	Mount St. Helens	Washington State	62
1985	Nevado del Ruiz	Armero, Colombia	22,000
1991	Pinatubo	Luzon, Philippines	200
1993	Mayon	Legazpi, Philippines	67

3. Use a world almanac to find the sites of major volcanic activity over the last 500 years.

4. Tack a large world map to your bulletin board. Using the data gathered by the teams, the data from the almanac, and the data in the table, mark the locations of volcanoes. Stick a red map pin on the map at the site of any volcanic eruption; stick a yellow map pin at the site of any active volcano.

5. Throughout the school year, keep adding to your records and to the world map. Record new volcanic activity and new eruptions as they occur. Note how the location of volcanoes is related to Earth's tectonic plates.

Analyze and Conclude

1. How many volcanic eruptions did you find in the news during the six months your team researched? What was the total number of eruptions found by your class during the two-year period?

2. Where on tectonic plates were the volcanoes located?

3. Were any of the volcanic eruptions on a mid-ocean ridge? What kind of an eruption did they have?

4. Hypothesize about the relationship between volcanic eruptions and Earth's tectonic plates.

Technology Link CD-ROM

INVESTIGATE FURTHER!

Use the **Science Processor CD-ROM**, *The Changing Earth* (Investigation 4, Thar She Blows) to learn about the different types of volcanoes and how they form. Plot volcanoes on a map and predict locations of other volcanoes.

Volcanoes and Plate Tectonics

Reading Focus What are volcanoes, and how are they classified?

Volcanoes

What comes to mind when you hear the word *volcano*? Probably you think of a large mountain spewing red-hot lava and other material high into Earth's atmosphere. Some volcanoes are like that. But a **volcano** is *any* opening in Earth's crust through which hot gases, rocks, and melted material erupt.

Have you ever opened a can of cold soda that has been dropped on the floor? Soda probably squirted into the air above the can. More soda bubbled out and flowed down the side of the can. Now, what do you think would happen if you opened a can of warm soda that had been dropped? The release of the warm soda from the can would be even *more* violent. Volcanoes are like cans of soda. Some erupt violently; others have more gentle eruptions.

The high temperatures and pressures deep within Earth can cause rock to melt. This melted rock is called **magma**. Because it's less dense than surrounding material, magma slowly makes its way toward Earth's surface. As it travels toward the surface, the magma melts surrounding material to form a central pipe, which is connected to the magma chamber. Eventually this hot molten material escapes through an opening in the crust

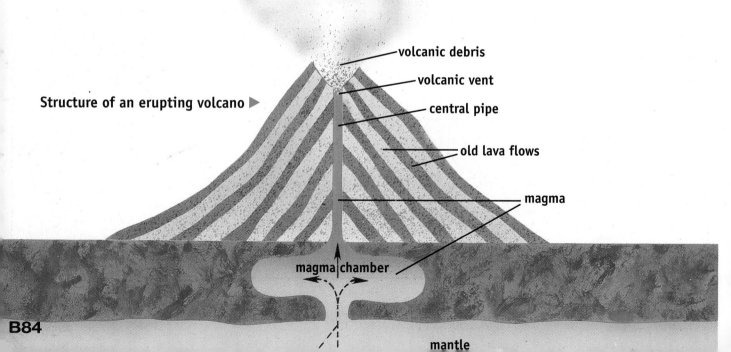

Structure of an erupting volcano ▶

volcanic debris
volcanic vent
central pipe
old lava flows
magma
magma chamber
mantle

▲ **Mount Tolbackik erupts in former U.S.S.R.**

▲ **Mount Kilauea erupts in Hawaii.**

called a volcanic vent. When magma reaches Earth's surface, it is called **lava**.

When lava flows from a volcano, its temperature can be higher than 1,100°C (2,012°F)! Lava is not the only kind of material that can be spewed from an erupting volcano. Solid volcanic debris includes bombs, cinders, ash, and dust. Bombs are volcanic rocks the size of a baseball or bigger. Large bombs can weigh nearly 100 metric tons (1,100 short tons). Volcanic dust and ash, on the other hand, range from about 0.25 mm to 0.5 mm (0.009 in. to 0.02 in.) in diameter and can be carried hundreds or thousands of kilometers from a volcano.

Volcanism and Plate Tectonics

Like earthquakes, volcanoes occur along certain plate boundaries. Many volcanoes occur around the edges of the Pacific Plate in an area that scientists have named the Ring of Fire (see map at right).

Volcanoes in the Ring of Fire were formed in subduction zones. In a subduction zone, plates collide and one plate descends below the other. The descending plate melts as it sinks slowly into the mantle. The magma then rises to the surface, forming a chain of volcanoes near the boundaries of the two plates.

Lava also erupts at divergent plate boundaries. Find the purple faults on the map. These indicate divergent plate

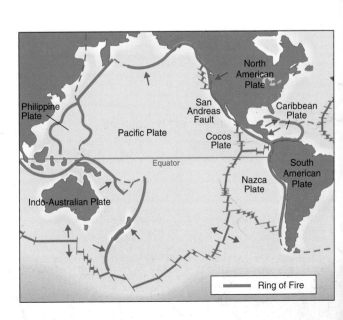

Between 500 and 600 active volcanoes make up the region called the Ring of Fire. ▶

CINDER CONE Paricutín, in Mexico (*left*); drawing of a cinder cone (*below*). Notice the very steep slopes.

vent

magma

layers of cinders

boundaries, where new ocean floor is formed as magma wells up between the separating plates.

Classifying Volcanoes

Volcanoes can be classified in different ways. One classification system is based on how often eruptions occur. An *active* volcano is one that erupts constantly. Some volcanoes that make up the Hawaiian Islands are active volcanoes. *Intermittent* volcanoes are those that erupt on a fairly regular basis. Mount Vesuvius, in Italy, is an intermittent volcano. Volcanoes that haven't erupted in a while but could erupt in the near future are called *dormant* volcanoes. Mount Lassen, in the California Cascade Range, is a dormant volcano. Volcanoes that have not erupted in recorded history are classified as *extinct* volcanoes. Mount Kenya, in Africa, is an extinct volcano.

Volcanoes can also be classified by the way they erupt. The way a volcano erupts depends on the type of lava that is ejected by the volcano. One type of lava

is a very hot fluid, which erupts quietly. Another kind of lava is thick and sticky. This sticky lava erupts violently.

The way a volcano erupts determines the shape of the mountain, or cone, that is produced. This shape can also be used to classify volcanoes. The three main types of volcanic cones—cinder, shield, and composite—are shown on these pages.

Cinder Cones

Cinders are sticky pea-sized bits of hardened lava. A **cinder cone** is made up of layers of cinders. The cinder cone forms around a central vent from which the cinders erupt.

These volcanic cones are produced by explosive eruptions. Generally, cinder cones are relatively small, less than 300 m (984 ft) tall, with very steep slopes. There is usually a bowl-shaped crater. Cinder cones often form in groups. Paricutín, a dormant volcano just west of Mexico City, and Stromboli, a very active volcano off the coast of Italy, are cinder-cone volcanoes.

Shield Cones

Shield cones form from lava that flows quietly from a crack in Earth's crust. What kind of lava do you think makes up a shield cone? Because of the composition of the lava, shield cones are large mountains that have very gentle slopes. Mauna Loa, the largest volcano on Earth, is a shield cone. Mauna Loa, which is a part of the island of Hawaii, towers over 4,100 m (13,448 ft) above sea level. The rest of this vast cone—about 5,000 m (16,400 ft)— is below the waters of the Pacific Ocean.

COMPOSITE CONE   Mount Fuji, in Japan (*top*); a drawing of a composite cone (*bottom*). This type of cone has steep slopes near its top and gentle slopes near its base.

Composite Cones

Composite cones form when explosive eruptions of sticky lava alternate with quieter eruptions of volcanic rock bits. Composite cones are also called stratovolcanoes. A composite cone has very steep slopes near its top but the slopes become gentler as you get closer to its base.

Composite cones are formed by the most explosive volcanoes. Their eruptions often occur without warning and can be very destructive. Mount Vesuvius, a once-dormant volcano in Italy, erupted in A.D. 79 and killed thousands of residents in Pompeii and nearby cities. This same volcano still erupts from time to time. You will learn more about Mount Vesuvius on pages B90–B91. ■

SHIELD CONE   Mauna Loa (*top*); a drawing of a shield cone (*bottom*). Notice the very gentle slopes.

Surtsey

Reading Focus Where is Earth's youngest volcano, and what can we learn from it?

▲ Surtsey, a young volcanic island, begins to form.

▲ Living things begin to populate the new island of Surtsey.

In 1963, off the southern coast of Iceland, a sailor on a fishing boat observed a pillar of smoke in the distance. He ran to alert his captain that he had spotted a ship that was on fire. Soon the odor of sulfur filled the salty air. The crew of the fishing vessel measured the water's temperature. It was much warmer than usual. The captain soon informed his crew that the smoke in the distance wasn't a burning ship at all. The smoke and fire signaled that one of the youngest volcanic islands on Earth was beginning to rise from the icy waters. Named after the Norse god Surtur, a giant who bore fire from the sea, Surtsey started to form as lava spewed from a long, narrow rift on the ocean floor.

Within a couple of weeks, an island nearly half a kilometer wide rose about 160 m (530 ft) above the water's surface. And after spewing lava, gases, and bits of rock debris from its vent for almost four years, Surtsey became inactive—geologically, that is. Scientists then had Surtsey designated as a nature preserve in order to study how living things inhabit a newly formed area. Today Surtsey is home to 27 species of plants and animals. Among the first organisms to inhabit the island were plants called sea rockets. Seeds from faraway places were carried to the island by birds and the wind. A few varieties of grasses and mosses painted colorful splotches against the black rock of the island. In the spring, seals now crawl up the black beaches to have their young.

Few people are allowed to visit this volcanic island. The Surtsey Research Council allows only a few scientists to visit the island to study the living things growing there. The impact of the few human beings that visit the island is very small. Only natural forces, such as wind and rain, have acted upon the land and its inhabitants. Erosion has shrunk the island to about three fourths of its original size. Unless it erupts again, the effects of wind and water will eventually make Surtsey disappear. ■

INVESTIGATE FURTHER!

RESEARCH

In 1973 a volcanic eruption occurred on Heimaey, an island off the southern coast of Iceland. Find out how much destruction occurred as a result of this eruption. Look also for ways that the eruption benefited the island. Compare the eruption on Heimaey with the eruption on Surtsey.

Science in Literature

ISLAND WITHOUT A PAST

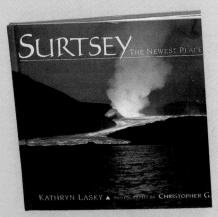

Surtsey: The Newest Place on Earth
by Kathryn Lasky
Photographs by Christopher G. Knight
Hyperion Books for Children, 1992

"This is the place where the animals have come one kind at a time—a bird, a seal, a fly. And often they have come alone, without a mate, at intervals over the years. This is the place where once upon a time was just twenty-nine years ago. This is the newest place on earth. This is Surtsey island."

Surtsey: The Newest Place on Earth by Kathryn Lasky combines the story of Surtsey with selections from ancient Icelandic mythology. As you read, you can also examine more than 40 photographs recording the formation of this island.

Mount Vesuvius

ITALY

MOUNT VESUVIUS

Reading Focus What is the impact of Mount Vesuvius on the people living nearby?

 **TIME Capsule**

Over the past 2,000 years or so, Mount Vesuvius, a cinder-cone volcano in southern Italy, has erupted about 50 times. Before its eruption in A.D. 79, Vesuvius was a picturesque cone-shaped mountain, towering over 1,000 m (3,300 ft) above the Bay of Naples. Vineyards and orchards crept nearly halfway up the mountain's slopes. Most historians think that very few people knew that Vesuvius was a volcano—until the fateful morning of August 24 in the year A.D. 79.

During the early-morning hours of that day, an earthquake rumbled through the area. By early afternoon loud thunder ripped through the air, and red-hot ash rained from the skies. Within 24 hours the twin Roman cities of Pompeii and Herculaneum were destroyed.

In the city of Pompeii, about 3,000 people were buried beneath about 5 to 8 m (16 to 26 ft) of volcanic ash. Because the ash was so hot and fell so quickly, it preserved many of the city's residents doing what they normally did in their day-to-day lives. By studying the remains of people, animals, utensils, and decorations found in Pompeii, archaeologists have learned a lot about the people who lived at that time. Archaeologists are scientists who study ancient cultures by digging up the evidence of human life from the past.

The city of Herculaneum, which was several kilometers from Pompeii, met its fate not from volcanic ash, such as that which buried Pompeii, but from a mudflow. A mudflow is a mixture of wet materials that rushes down a mountainside and destroys everything in its path. Volcanologists, or scientists who study volcanoes, think that flowing hot volcanic debris swept over the city and covered it to depths of over 20 m (66 ft)!

The eruption of Mount Vesuvius in A.D. 79 is probably most famous because

◀ **Cast of man buried by the eruption of Mount Vesuvius (far left); nuts buried and preserved by the eruption (left).**

it perfectly preserved the people and customs of ancient Rome. However, it was not the last or the worst eruption in the area. In the summer of 1631, earthquakes once again shook the area. By winter, molten rock filled the volcano. On December 16, 1631, ash was spewing from the mountain. By the next day, red-hot lava raced down the volcano's slopes. The destructive toll of this eruption included 15 villages. At least 4,000 people and 6,000 animals died.

Since the 1631 eruption of Mount Vesuvius, the volcano has erupted every 15 to 40 years. The ash and rock fragments have made the soil very fertile. Farmers successfully grow grapes, citrus fruits, carnations, beans, and peas in this region. But the threat of losing it all to the volcano is always there. ■

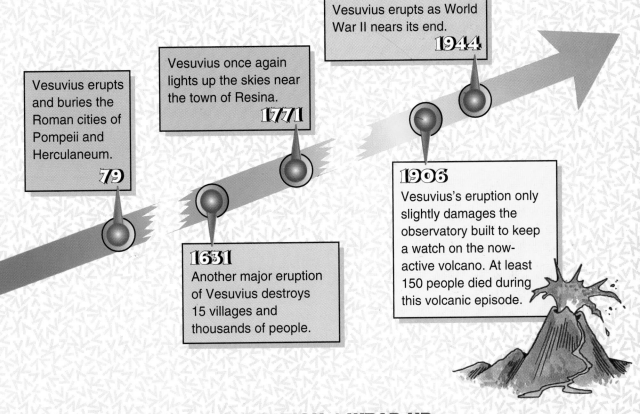

Vesuvius erupts and buries the Roman cities of Pompeii and Herculaneum.
79

Vesuvius once again lights up the skies near the town of Resina.
1771

Vesuvius erupts as World War II nears its end.
1944

1631
Another major eruption of Vesuvius destroys 15 villages and thousands of people.

1906
Vesuvius's eruption only slightly damages the observatory built to keep a watch on the now-active volcano. At least 150 people died during this volcanic episode.

INVESTIGATION 1 WRAP-UP

THINK IT WRITE IT

REVIEW

1. Describe how most volcanoes form.

2. Make a chart that compares and contrasts cinder cones, shield cones, and composite cones. Include a sketch of each type of volcano.

CRITICAL THINKING

3. Imagine you are visiting Surtsey with a group of scientists. Write a diary entry describing what you see.

4. How might Surtsey have developed differently if tourism had been allowed?

HOW DO VOLCANIC ERUPTIONS AFFECT EARTH?

In March 1980, a strong earthquake rocked Mount St. Helens, in the state of Washington. For the next two months, steam and ash blew out. Then in May the volcano exploded with great violence. In this investigation you'll find out what you can expect before, during, and after a volcanic eruption.

Activity

Volcanoes You Can Eat!

How is an erupting volcano like a pot of cooking oatmeal? Volcanoes erupt because materials are forced out of a hole, called a vent. Can you see a vent in a pot of oatmeal?

Procedure

1. Use a measuring cup to measure the amounts of quick oats and water shown in the picture.

> See **SCIENCE** and **MATH TOOLBOX** page H7 if you need to review **Measuring Volume.**

2. Pour the oats and water into a saucepan and mix together.

Step 4

3. Using an oven mitt, place the saucepan on a hot plate and set the hot plate on *Medium High*.

4. After the hot plate has warmed up, stir the oats and water constantly for one minute.

5. Carefully observe the top surface of the oatmeal as it cooks. Record your observations in your *Science Notebook*.

6. After one minute, turn off the hot plate. Remove the oatmeal from the heat.

Analyze and Conclude

1. What did you observe on the surface of the oatmeal as it cooked?

2. How is cooking oatmeal like an erupting volcano? How is it different?

3. What, do you think, would happen if you covered the pot and continued to heat the mixture? What kind of volcano would be modeled?

UNIT PROJECT LINK

Have you ever dreamed of living on your own island paradise? Locate the Ring of Fire on a map and identify those islands created by volcanic activity. Predict where future volcanic islands might rise out of the ocean; indicate these areas on your map. Draw a small picture of your island paradise and describe where you think your island will emerge.

Technology Link

For more help with your Unit Project, go to **www.eduplace.com**.

Mount Pinatubo

MOUNT PINATUBO

THE PHILIPPINES

Reading Focus What are some of the long-term effects of the eruption of Mount Pinatubo?

Mount Pinatubo, which towers more than 1,900 m (6,200 ft) above sea level, is only one of about 13 active volcanoes in the Philippines. This volcano, which is located on the island of Luzon, is a composite cone. At times when it erupts, there is a sticky lava flow. At other times a combination of ash, dust, and other volcanic rock bits erupt.

Mount Pinatubo and the other volcanoes in the Philippines formed as a result of tectonic activity. The Philippine Islands are a part of the Ring of Fire.

You already know that at some convergent plate boundaries, one oceanic plate collides with another oceanic plate. At such boundaries, one plate goes down deep into Earth's mantle. As the plate is dragged down, it bends, and a deep canyon, or ocean trench, forms. As this oceanic plate descends into the asthenosphere, parts of the plate melt, forming magma. The magma then rises and forms a chain of volcanoes called **island arcs**. The islands that make up the Philippines are a mature island arc system that formed long ago when two oceanic plates collided.

There She Blows!

After being dormant for over six centuries, Mount Pinatubo began to erupt in mid-June of 1991. As the eruption began, brilliant lightning bolts colored the skies above the volcano. Within minutes, these same skies were black because of the enormous amounts of ash, dust, and gases that spurted from the mountain. Scientists estimate that the mountain's violent eruption had a force equal to that of 2,000 to 3,000 exploding atomic bombs! The ash clouds produced by the eruption polluted the air so much that astronauts in space aboard the space shuttle could not get a clear view of Earth's surface!

This period of volcanic activity lasted for several months and stopped in early September 1991. The first eruption destroyed about 42,000 houses and

Two oceanic plates colliding ▼

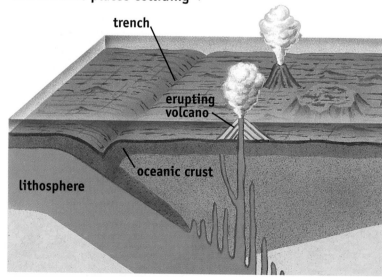

trench

erupting volcano

oceanic crust

lithosphere

nearly 100,000 acres of farm-land. Over 900 people died. Much of the damage and many of the deaths were caused by flowing mud and hot volcanic material. Also, masses of gas, ash, and igneous rock called pumice covered many villages at and near the base of Mount Pinatubo.

The cause of the 1991 eruption of Mount Pinatubo is not completely understood. It is likely that many months prior to the eruption, magma began forcing its way up through the lithosphere. Slowly the magma made its way toward the surface. As it snaked along its path, the magma increased temperatures and pressures beneath the mountain. In some places the magma crept into cracks in the bedrock, causing the bedrock to swell. On June 15, 1991, the mountain erupted, sending clouds of gases and tons of lava to Earth's surface.

Mount Pinatubo's Warning Signs

Earthquakes and volcanoes are more common in some parts of the world than in others. Both are closely related to the

JUNE 19–27, 1991

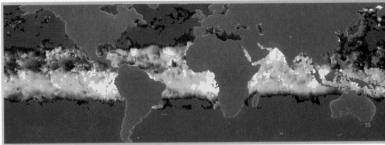

AUGUST 8–14, 1991

Effect of the eruption of Mount Pinatubo. The yellow band shows how volcanic debris travels around the globe and extends over time. About how many weeks have elapsed from one image to the next?

movements of tectonic plates. Scientists monitor earthquake- and volcano-prone areas for changes. But the exact time of volcanic eruptions can be difficult to predict accurately. However, in the case of Mount Pinatubo, the volcanic mountain "cooperated." There were many warnings of its explosive 1991 eruption.

First, there was an earthquake that shook the area in July 1990. There is

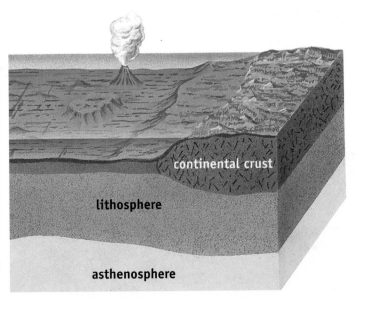

continental crust

lithosphere

asthenosphere

INVESTIGATE FURTHER!

RESEARCH

Find out about another famous volcano in the Philippines called Mount Mayon. Where is it located? How do you think this volcano formed? When did it last erupt? What kind of volcano is it?

is produced when sticky lava is slowly squeezed from a volcano's vent, had doubled in size in a little over two months!

Because the volcano gave these warning signs, many lives were saved. For several months before the explosion, scientists explained what the mountain was doing and urged people to leave the area. Over 200,000 people had been safely evacuated from the area before the explosion occurred.

What Goes Up Must Come Down— But When?

Before the eruption, instruments aboard weather satellites monitored the atmosphere above the volcano. These instruments were looking for increases in the amount of sulfur dioxide in the air around the composite cone. About two weeks before the explosion, the amount of sulfur dioxide was ten times what it had been the month before. This increase

often a relationship between earthquake activity and later volcanic activity. In April 1991, small clouds of smoke and ash were forced from cracks along the mountain's slopes. These clouds prompted earth scientists from the Philippines and the United States to more closely monitor the majestic Pinatubo.

Watching Pinatubo

Two kinds of measuring devices—seismometers and tiltmeters—were put into place near the mountain and then connected to computers. A **seismometer** is an instrument that detects Earth's movements. These movements can indicate that a volcano is preparing to blow its top! A **tiltmeter** measures any change in the slope of an area. Installing these devices allowed scientists to note any bulges that formed in the mountain's slopes. Such bulges indicate the presence of magma and gases welling up into the volcano. In fact, Mount Pinatubo did bulge before the 1991 eruption. Its lava dome, a bulge that

Evacuation of people before the eruption of Mount Pinatubo ▶

was another warning that Mount Pinatubo might be ready to erupt.

These same instruments measured the amount of sulfur dioxide that had been spewed out into the air during the eruption. About 15 to 20 million tons of this gas blew nearly 40 km (25 mi) into the air! This volcanic gas combined with other gases in the air and formed a thin layer of sulfuric acid droplets that circled the globe within about three weeks.

Mount Pinatubo, like other active volcanoes, is a source of pollution. The dust, gases, and ash spewed out in 1991 have effected Earth and its atmosphere. First, soon after the eruption, vivid sunsets colored the skies in many places far removed from the Philippines.

Second, the sulfuric acid droplets remained above the planet for a few years after the eruption. The droplets reflected back into space about 2 percent of the Sun's energy that normally reached Earth's surface. This in turn led to a global cooling of about 1°C (1.8°F). This short period of cooling reversed a global warming trend for a short time. The warming trend is caused by the collection of gases

▲ **Sunset after the 1991 eruption of Mount Pinatubo**

that trap the Sun's heat. Called the greenhouse effect, it is the result of natural climatic changes and human activities, such as burning fossil fuels and cutting down forests.

Another effect of the 1991 eruption of Mount Pinatubo is that the 30 to 40 million tons of sulfuric acid added to the air may speed up the breakdown of Earth's ozone layer. The ozone layer in the upper atmosphere protects you and Earth's other inhabitants from harmful solar rays. ■

INVESTIGATION 2 WRAP-UP

REVIEW

1. What are some long-term effects of volcanic eruptions? Use Mount Pinatubo as an example.

2. What events may occur before a volcanic eruption?

CRITICAL THINKING

3. Explain the process that creates island arcs.

4. You have just invented a tool that can accurately predict a volcano. Write a short paragraph to convince scientists to use it.

IN WHAT OTHER PLACES CAN VOLCANOES OCCUR?

So far, you have learned that volcanoes can occur along mid-ocean ridges and where one tectonic plate is descending under another. In this investigation you'll explore two other kinds of places where volcanoes can occur.

Activity

How Hawaii Formed

Geologists have a hypothesis that magma rising from a large chamber of molten rock—called a hot spot—deep below the Pacific Plate has built the volcanic islands that make up the state of Hawaii. In this activity you'll examine some of their evidence.

MATERIALS
- metric ruler
- map of the Hawaiian Islands, showing volcanoes
- calculator
- *Science Notebook*

Procedure

1. Measure the distance between the center of the island of Hawaii and the center of each of the other islands. Record this information in your *Science Notebook*. Use the scale on the map to find out how far apart the centers are.

Math Hint *To determine the youngest and oldest islands, compare the same place values.*

2. The table on this page tells you the estimated age of the rock on each island. Record the youngest island and the oldest island.

The Hawaiian Islands	
Island	**Estimated Age of Rock**
Maui	1.63 million years
Molokai	1.84 million years
Oahu	2.9 million years
Kauai	5.1 million years
Hawaii	375,000 years
Lanai	1.28 million years
Niihau	5.5 million years
Kahoolawe	1.03 million years

Kauai

Mount Waialeale

Niihau

Oahu

Diamond Head

Molokai

Maui

Lanai

Kahoolawe

Haleakala

Pacific Ocean

N

Hawaii

Mauna Loa

HAWAIIAN ISLANDS

0   30 mi
0   50 km

▲ Mountain Peaks

▲ The Hawaiian Islands

3. **Make a chart** that shows the age difference between Hawaii and each of the other islands.

See **SCIENCE** *and* **MATH TOOLBOX** *page H4 if you need to review* **Using a Calculator.**

Analyze and Conclude

1. Based on your measurements, what is the distance between Hawaii and Kauai?

2. Which island is the youngest? Which is the oldest?

3. If the hot spot stays in the same place and the Pacific Plate moves over it, the hot spot may have created one island after another. Based on the ages of the islands, in which direction is the Pacific Plate moving?

4. Based on the ages of Hawaii and Kauai, what was the speed of the plate's movement?

5. What can you **infer** about the speed at which the Pacific Plate moves—does it move at a constant speed or does its speed change from time to time?

INVESTIGATE FURTHER!

RESEARCH

Look at a map of Earth's surface features. Observe the northwestward underwater extension of the Hawaiian Islands. Notice that there is an abrupt northward bend where the Hawaiian chain meets the Emperor Seamount chain. What do you think this bend means?

ASIA
NORTH AMERICA
HAWAIIAN ISLANDS
Pacific Ocean

An Island in the Making

Midway

Reading Focus What happens when a volcano occurs in the middle of a tectonic plate?

Hot Spots

Recall that the theory of plate tectonics states that slabs of Earth's crust and upper mantle move slowly over the planet's surface. Convection currents in the partly melted mantle, or asthenosphere, are thought to drive plate motion.

Most of Earth's volcanoes are found along convergent and divergent plate boundaries. But recently, scientists discovered that volcanoes can also form in the middle of a tectonic plate. **Hot spots** are extremely hot places deep within Earth's mantle. The magma that forms at these spots slowly rises toward the surface because the magma is less dense than the surrounding material. Scientists have evidence that most of the 120 known hot spots don't move. Rather, as a plate moves over a hot spot, the magma wells up and breaks through the crust to form a volcano, as shown in the drawings on this page.

Formation of the Hawaiian Islands

Pele is the mythical goddess of Hawaiian volcanoes. Native legends state that volcanic eruptions along the island chain are caused when the goddess is angry. She supposedly takes her Pa'oa, a magic stick, and pokes it into the ground, unearthing the fires below.

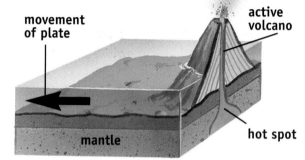

movement of plate — active volcano — hot spot — mantle

1 As a plate passes over a hot spot, a volcano is formed.

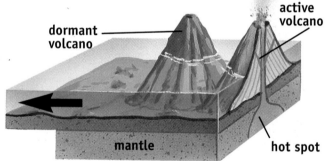

dormant volcano — active volcano — mantle — hot spot

2 When the plate moves, the old volcano becomes dormant. A new volcano forms over the hot spot and becomes active.

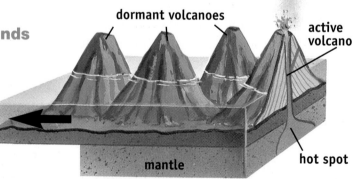

dormant volcanoes — active volcano — mantle — hot spot

3 The plate keeps moving, and the process continues.

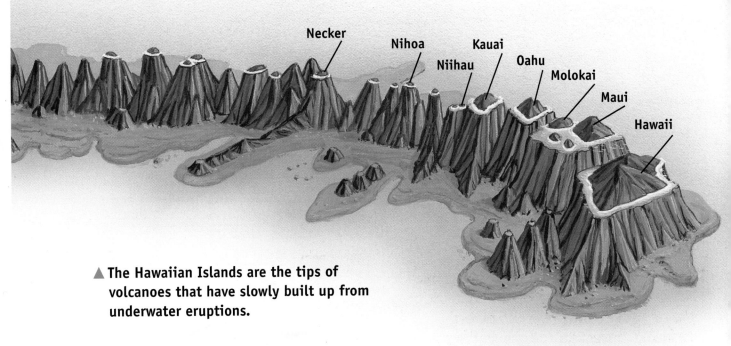

▲ The Hawaiian Islands are the tips of volcanoes that have slowly built up from underwater eruptions.

▲ Pele

The islands are said to have been formed when Pele and her sister, Namakaokahai, had a bitter argument. As the sisters quarreled, Pele moved from island to island and dug fire pits—the Hawaiian volcanoes themselves. Pele is said to have first used her Pa'oa on Kauai. Then she fled to Oahu, Molokai, Maui, and finally to the "Big Island," Hawaii. Legend says that Pele now lives at the summit of Kilauea on Hawaii.

Scientists have evidence that the Hawaiian Islands formed as the Pacific Plate slowly moved northwestward over a hot spot beneath the Pacific Ocean. A chain of volcanic islands, each developing as the plate moved over the hot spot on the ocean floor, formed over millions of years. This chain of islands, which is made up of over 80 large volcanoes, is called the Hawaiian Ridge–Emperor Seamount Chain. A seamount is a volcanic peak that rises at least 1,000 m (3,300 ft) above the ocean floor. The Emperor Seamounts, which now lie beneath the ocean's surface, were once islands. They have been eroded by wind and waves. The oldest seamount in the chain is 74 million years old.

The Hawaiian Ridge–Emperor Seamount Chain stretches northwest from the island of Hawaii and then north to the Aleutian Trench, off the coast of Kamchatka. The Hawaiian Ridge segment alone, which includes the Hawaiian Islands, is about 2,560 km (1,540 mi) long! Scientists estimate that the amount of lava thrust out to form this volcanic ridge was enough to cover the entire state of California with a blanket of lava 1.6 km (1 mi) thick!

Internet Field Trip

Visit **www.eduplace.com** to see an illustration of Earth's crust, mantle, and core.

◀ DSV *Sea Cliff*, used to study underwater volcanoes

Loihi—A New Island in the Making

The Hawaiian hot spot, which lies deep beneath the Pacific Ocean floor, currently feeds the volcanoes Mauna Loa and Kilauea on the island of Hawaii.

Recently a new seamount was discovered, forming off the southern coast of Hawaii. This underwater volcano, or seamount, is called Loihi (lō ē'hē). Loihi towers about 3,300 m (10,900 ft) above the ocean floor. Only about 1,000 m (3,300 ft) of salty water covers this young volcano.

Scientists don't expect Loihi to poke above the water's surface for at least another 50,000 years. To study the newly emerging member of the Hawaiian chain, scientists have used a submarine, the DSV *Sea Cliff*, to take pictures of the events as they unfold.

Photographs of Loihi taken by cameras aboard the submarine show fresh pillow lavas and talus blocks. Pillow lava is lava formed when there is an undersea eruption. The rock formed is rounded, looking somewhat like piles of pillows. Pillow lavas form when the extremely hot lava erupts into the cold ocean waters, which quickly cool the lava. Talus blocks, which are also linked with "fresh" eruptions, are large angular pieces of rock that slide down a mountain's slope and pile up at the base of the structure.

Maps made of the area surrounding the new volcano show that Loihi is similar to some of its sister volcanoes—Mauna Loa and Kilauea. It is gently sloping and has a flat top. A **caldera** (kal dər'ə), or large circular depression, with a diameter of about 5 km (3 mi) lies within the volcano's summit. Cracking, followed by the formation of new ocean crust, is occurring along the sides of the volcano. The exact age of this new volcano is not yet known. Scientists have hypothesized, though, that the volcano is only a few hundred years old.

Within a few years, scientists are hoping to get an even better view of Loihi. They plan to use optical cables to monitor the eruptions taking place as they happen. These cables will connect an underwater observatory with an onshore observatory. The cables will then transmit information from the various instruments monitoring the volcano. Seismometers will also be put in place near the volcano.

The caldera of a volcano ▶

Perhaps even a small submarine rover will crawl around the ocean floor to witness history in the making!

Risk of Eruptions

Because the eruptions of the Hawaiian volcanoes are quiet flows, scientists have been able to study these volcanoes at close range without much danger. In fact, the volcanoes that make up the islands of Hawaii are probably some of the most closely studied volcanoes in the world. Look at the map showing the risk of volcanic eruptions in Hawaii. Which part of the Big Island seems to be the most dangerous? Why?

Perhaps because they are two of the youngest and most active volcanoes in the Hawaiian Ridge chain, Mauna Loa and Kilauea are closely watched. Study the bar graphs below. Which of the two volcanoes has erupted more often? ■

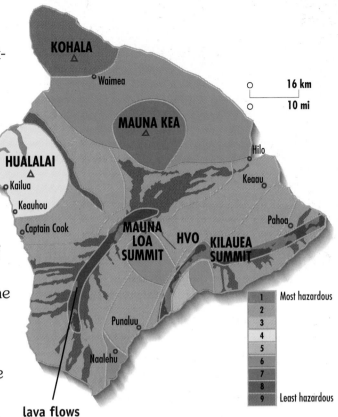

▲ Map of Hawaii, showing risk of volcanic eruptions

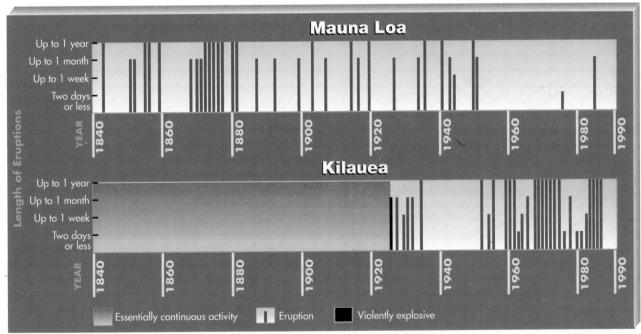

The graphs compare the eruption histories of Mauna Loa and Kilauea since 1840. State two conclusions you can draw from these bar graphs.

Using Robots to Investigate Volcanoes

Reading Focus How do computers help scientists study volcanoes?

What has eight legs and a "nerve cord" that sends and receives messages, is over 3 m (10 ft) tall, weighs about 772 kg (1,700 lb), and costs nearly $2 million? Give up? It's Dante, one of a series of robots designed by computer scientists at Carnegie-Mellon University, in Pittsburgh, Pennsylvania.

Dante II exploring a volcano in Anchorage, Alaska ▼

Dante was named after a fourteenth-century poet who wrote an epic poem in which he spends some time traveling through the fiery regions deep within Earth. During part of his mythical journey, Dante is led by a ghost named Virgil. Because the scientists send their robots into the fiery depths of volcanoes, they thought it appropriate to name the robots Dante. A robot called Virgil carries Dante along some stretches of its journeys.

The first version of Dante was designed to help volcanologists explore one of the most active volcanoes on Earth—Mount Erebus, a smoldering 3,790-m (12,500-ft) volcano on Antarctica. A kink in one of the robot's cables, however, stopped the robot from going deeper than 6 m (about 20 ft) into the volcano. Although it couldn't complete its mission, Dante proved that it could tackle similar future assignments.

Dante II made its debut in Anchorage, Alaska, where scientists used this improved robot to explore Alaska's Mount Spurr. Dante II descended slowly but surely 100 m (330 ft) into the volcano. It produced a three-dimensional map of the rugged terrain of the crater's floor. Dante II also collected and analyzed gases being emitted from the volcano. Scientists used the information to infer that Mount Spurr will probably remain dormant for some time.

The Amazing Dante II, A Volcano-Exploring Robot

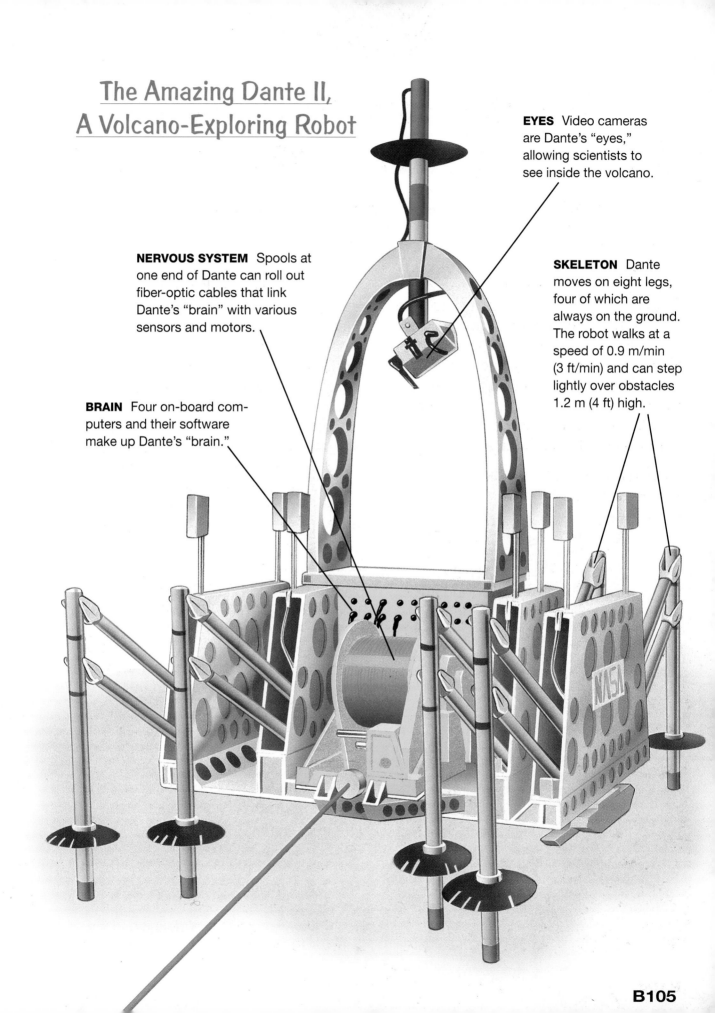

EYES Video cameras are Dante's "eyes," allowing scientists to see inside the volcano.

NERVOUS SYSTEM Spools at one end of Dante can roll out fiber-optic cables that link Dante's "brain" with various sensors and motors.

SKELETON Dante moves on eight legs, four of which are always on the ground. The robot walks at a speed of 0.9 m/min (3 ft/min) and can step lightly over obstacles 1.2 m (4 ft) high.

BRAIN Four on-board computers and their software make up Dante's "brain."

Great Rift Valley of Africa

Reading Focus Where in Africa is the Great Rift Valley, and what makes it special to scientists?

Rifting

What happens if you slowly pull on some silicon putty? At first the putty stretches and sags. Eventually the putty breaks. The process of rifting is similar to the stretching and breaking of the putty.

Rifting is a process that occurs at divergent plate boundaries. As two plates separate, hot magma in the asthenosphere oozes upward to fill the newly formed gap. In general, rifting occurs along mid-ocean ridges deep beneath the oceans. Rifting along mid-ocean ridges leads to the process of sea-floor spreading. Some rifting, however, occurs where two continental plates are moving apart. When rifting occurs on land, the continental crust breaks up, or splits. Study

the drawings on these two pages. What eventually forms when rifting occurs in continental crust?

The Great African Rift System

Over the past 25 million to 30 million years, continental rifting has been pulling eastern Africa apart—at the rate of several centimeters per decade. Jokes a Djibouti geologist, "[We are] Africa's fastest-growing nation!" Three rifts—the East African Rift, one in the Gulf of Aden, and a third in the Red Sea—form a system 5,600 km (3,472 mi) long known as the Great Rift Valley. The place where the three rift systems meet is called the Afar Triangle, named after the people who live in the region.

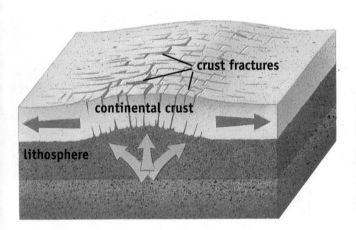

1 Magma produced by Earth's mantle rises through the crust, lifts it up, and causes fractures in the crust.

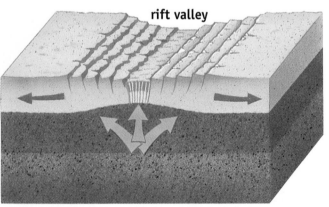

2 The crust pulls apart, faults open, and blocks of crust fall inward. Volcanoes begin to erupt. A rift valley forms.

The Great Rift Valley runs through Mozambique, Zambia, Zaire, Tanzania, Uganda, Kenya, and Sudan, up into the Ethiopian highlands and down into the Djibouti coastal plains. It is the place where humans had their first encounters with volcanoes. In fact, it is because of volcanic eruptions that anthropologists today are finding very old human remains. Some human ancestors living in the Afar region of Africa were buried under the volcanic debris of an eruption that occurred millions of years ago! Their fossil remains continue to be unearthed, and they provide important information about where early humans lived.

Found along the Great Rift Valley are some of the world's oldest volcanoes—including Mount Kenya and Mount Kilimanjaro. Mount Kilimanjaro, a volcano that towers nearly 5,900 m (19,500 ft) above the surrounding land, is Africa's highest peak.

Rifting along the Great Rift Valley has produced some of Earth's deepest lakes as well as some of the highest volcanic mountains. Lake Tanganyika, the longest freshwater lake on Earth, is the second

deepest lake in the world. It formed millions of years ago when two tectonic plates shifted horizontally.

All along the Great Rift Valley, as with any rift zone, earthquakes and volcanoes are common. Study the map on page B108. Notice that along the East African

Mount Kilimanjaro compared to Lake Tanganyika

Height/Depth (in meters)

6000
5000
4000 — Mount Kilimanjaro
3000
2000
1000
Sea Level
-1000 — Lake Tanganyika
-2000

Using Math *About how many times higher is Mount Kilimanjaro than Lake Tanganyika is deep?*

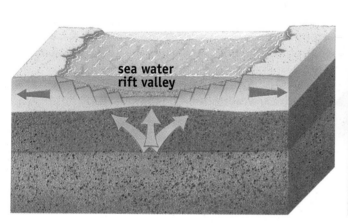

3 The rift valley widens, allowing sea water to fill the basin that has formed.

sea water
rift valley

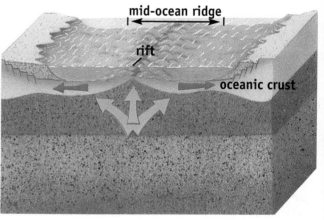

4 A new rift begins in the middle of the ocean basin that was formed. This rift is known as a mid-ocean ridge.

mid-ocean ridge
rift
oceanic crust

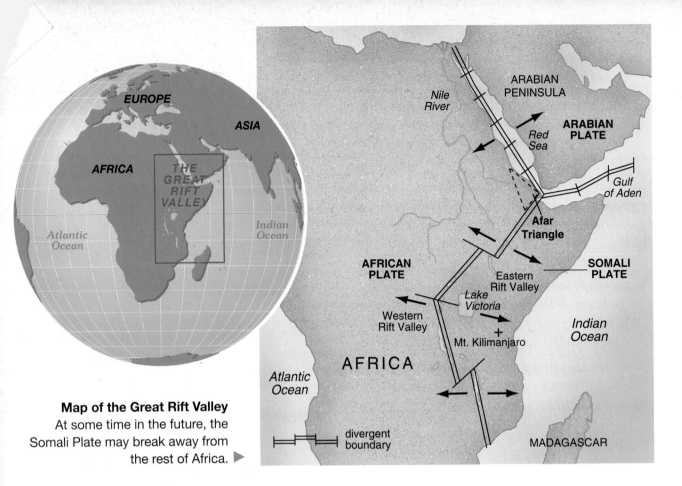

Map of the Great Rift Valley
At some time in the future, the Somali Plate may break away from the rest of Africa. ▶

Rift, the Somali Plate is moving away from the African Plate. Along the Gulf of Aden arm of the rift, the Somali Plate is moving southeastward relative to the Arabian Plate. How might this area look 30 million years from now if rifting continues?

As with most volcanic areas, fertile soils cover much of the land in the Great Rift Valley. In Kenya, for example, rich red soils blanket the land. Trona, a mineral in the local volcanic ash, is used to make glass and detergents.

Near the Afar Triangle, where Earth's crust is only 25 km (15.5 mi) thick, steam from the many volcanoes spouts into the air. Someday, perhaps, the volcanoes of the rift system will provide electricity from geothermal energy to Africa. ∎

INVESTIGATION 3 WRAP-UP

REVIEW

1. Volcanoes occur on the surface of Earth's crust; yet, scientists study volcanoes to find out about the mantle. Explain.

2. Describe how volcanic islands can occur in places other than at plate boundaries.

CRITICAL THINKING

3. Write your own legend to explain the volcanic eruptions in Hawaii.

4. Suppose you are a volcanologist. Explain how fiber-optic cables will be used to get a better view of Loihi.

REFLECT & EVALUATE

Word Power

Write the letter of the term that best matches the definition. *Not all terms will be used*.

1. Extremely hot places deep within Earth's mantle
2. Any opening in Earth's crust through which hot gases, rocks, and melted material erupt
3. Process of hot magma oozing upward to fill a new gap formed by separating plates
4. Formed when lava flows quietly from a crack in Earth's crust
5. An instrument that detects Earth's movements
6. Magma that has reached Earth's surface

a. cinder cone
b. composite cone
c. hot spots
d. lava
e rifting
f. seismometer
g. shield cone
h. volcano

Check What You Know

Write the word in each pair that correctly completes each sentence.

1. (Dormant, Intermittent) volcanoes haven't erupted in a while, but could erupt in the near future.
2. A short-term global (cooling, warming) resulted from Mount Pinatubo.
3. The islands of Hawaii were created by the moving of a plate over a (hot spot, rift valley).

Problem Solving

1. How are volcanoes on spreading ridges and rift zones different from those above descending edges of ocean plates?
2. On a map of Earth's tectonic plates, show where volcanoes are most likely to occur and explain why. Identify five active volcanoes throughout the world.

BUILD YOUR PORTFOLIO

Make a copy of this drawing. Add an arrow to show which direction the Pacific Plate is moving. Then use the drawing to explain how the Hawaiian Islands formed.

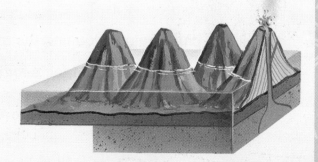

Using READING SKILLS

Main Idea and Details

When you read science, it's important to recognize which facts and details support or explain the main idea. First identify the main idea by looking for clues such as a title or a topic sentence that states the main idea. Then look for statements that support that idea.

> Look for clues to find the main idea.
>
> Look for statements, facts, and details that support the main idea.

Read the paragraphs below. Then complete the exercises that follow.

Earth as a Magnet

Earth is like a giant magnet, and it has two magnetic poles. These poles are inclined, or tilted, about 11° from the geographic poles. The magnetic field around Earth is thought to be due to movements within Earth's fluid outer core, which is composed mainly of iron and nickel. For reasons unknown, Earth's magnetic field sometimes reverses itself. This is called a **magnetic reversal**.

At present, the magnetic field is said to be normal. This means that the north-seeking needle of a compass will point toward Earth's north magnetic pole.

1. Write the letter of the sentence that states the main idea of the paragraphs.

   a. Earth's outer core is fluid.

   b. Earth is like a giant magnet with two magnetic poles.

   c. Earth's magnetic field is normal at present.

   d. Scientists don't know why Earth's magnetic field sometimes reverses itself.

2. What clues helped you find the main idea?

3. List the most important facts and details that support the main idea.

 **Bar Graph**

This bar graph shows the heights of various volcanoes. Each height has been rounded to the nearest 50 meters.

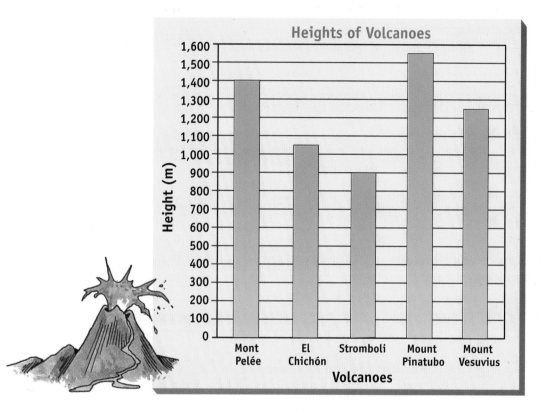

Use the data in the bar graph to complete the exercises.

1. Which volcano's height is the median?

2. What is the estimated range of heights?

3. How does the range of the volcano heights compare to the median height?

4. The height of which volcano is 500 m less than the height of Mont Pelée?

5. Do the data have a mode? Tell why or why not.

6. About how many kilometers tall is Stromboli?

7. Suppose a volcano that is not shown on the graph has a height of 1,060 m. Which volcano on the graph has the same height?

WRAP-UP!

On your own, use scientific methods to investigate a question about the changing Earth.

THINK LIKE A SCIENTIST

Ask a Question

Pose a question about Earth changes and their effects. For example, ask, "How can columns that support buildings and roadways be made more resistant to earthquakes?"

Make a Hypothesis

Suggest a hypothesis that is a possible answer to the question. One hypothesis is that the columns could be made stronger or more flexible in some way.

Plan and Do a Test

Plan a controlled experiment to find out what type of materials would make support columns more resistant to earthquakes. You could start with plaster of Paris, cardboard or plastic tubes to use as column molds, and different materials to make your model columns stronger—or stronger and more flexible. Develop a procedure that uses these materials to test the hypothesis. With permission, carry out your experiment. Follow the safety guidelines on pages S14–S15.

Record and Analyze

Observe carefully and record your data accurately. Make repeated observations.

Draw Conclusions

Look for evidence to support the hypothesis or to show that it is false. Draw conclusions about the hypothesis. Repeat the experiment to verify the results.

WRITING IN SCIENCE
Research Report

Research information about earthquakes and what scientists have learned about where they occur. Present your findings in a research report. Use these guidelines to prepare your report.

- Gather information from several sources, including the Internet.
- Keep track of each source, page reference, and Web site.
- Organize the information into main categories.
- Draw a conclusion from your research.

SCIENCE and MATH TOOLBOX

Using a Microscope

A microscope makes it possible to see very small things by magnifying them. Some microscopes have a set of lenses that magnify objects by different amounts.

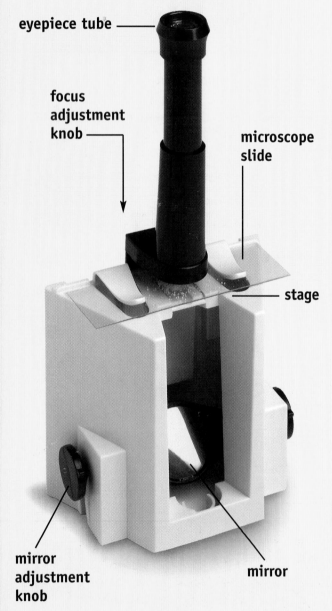

eyepiece tube

focus adjustment knob

microscope slide

stage

mirror adjustment knob

mirror

Examine Some Salt Grains

Handle a microscope carefully; it can break easily. Carry it firmly with both hands and avoid touching the lenses.

1. Turn the mirror toward a source of light. **NEVER** use the Sun as a light source.

2. Place a few grains of salt on the slide. Put the slide on the stage of the microscope.

3. Bring the salt grains into focus. Turn the adjustment knob on the back of the microscope as you look through the eyepiece.

4. Raise the eyepiece tube to increase the magnification; lower it to decrease magnification.

Salt grains magnified one hundred times (100X)

Making a Bar Graph

A bar graph helps you organize and compare data. For example, you might want to make a bar graph to compare weather data for different places.

Make a Bar Graph of Annual Snowfall

For more than 20 years, the cities listed in the table have been recording their yearly snowfall. The table shows the average number of centimeters of snow that the cities receive each year. Use the data in the table to make a bar graph showing the cities' average annual snowfall.

Snowfall	
City	Snowfall (cm)
Atlanta, GA	5
Charleston, SC	1.5
Houston, TX	1
Jackson, MS	3
New Orleans, LA	0.5
Tucson, AZ	3

1. Title your graph. The title should help a reader understand what your graph describes.

2. Choose a scale and mark equal intervals. The vertical scale should include the least value and the greatest value in the set of data.

3. Label the vertical axis *Snowfall (cm)* and the horizontal axis *City*. Space the city names equally.

4. Carefully graph the data. Depending on the interval you choose, some amounts may be between two numbers.

5. Check each step of your work.

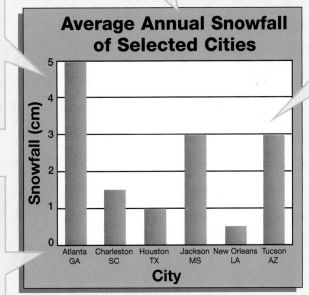

Average Annual Snowfall of Selected Cities

Using a Calculator

After you've made measurements, a calculator can help you analyze your data. Some calculators have a memory key that allows you to save the result of one calculation while you do another.

Add and Divide to Find Percent

The table shows the amount of rain that was collected using a rain gauge in each month of one year. You can use a calculator to help you find the total yearly rainfall. Then you can find the percent of rain that fell during January.

1. Add the numbers. When you add a series of numbers, you need not press the equal sign until the last number is entered. Just press the plus sign after you enter each number (except the last).

2. If you make a mistake while you are entering numbers, press the clear entry (CE/C) key to erase your mistake. Then you can continue entering the rest of the numbers you are adding. If you can't fix your mistake, you can press the (CE/C) key once or twice until the screen shows 0. Then start over.

3. Your total should be 1,131. Now clear the calculator until the screen shows 0. Then divide the rainfall amount for January by the total yearly rainfall (1,131). Press the percent (%) key. Then press the equal sign key.

214 ÷ 1131 % =

The percent of yearly rainfall that fell in January is 18.921309, which rounds to 19%.

Rainfall	
Month	**Rain (mm)**
Jan.	214
Feb.	138
Mar.	98
Apr.	157
May	84
June	41
July	5
Aug.	23
Sept.	48
Oct.	75
Nov.	140
Dec.	108

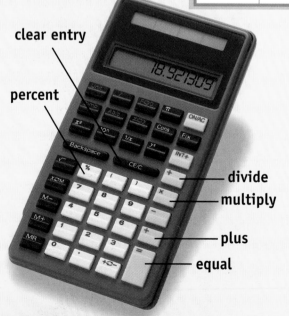

clear entry

percent

divide

multiply

plus

equal

Finding an
Average

An average is a way to describe a set of data using one number. For example, you could compare the surface temperature of several stars that are of the same type. You could find the average surface temperature of these stars.

Add and Divide to Find the Average

Suppose scientists found the surface temperature of eight blue-white stars to be those shown in the table. What is the average surface temperature of the stars listed?

Surface Temperature of Selected Blue-white Stars

Blue-white Star	Surface Temperature (°F)
1	7,200
2	6,100
3	6,000
4	6,550
5	7,350
6	6,800
7	7,500
8	6,300

1. First find the sum of the data. Add the numbers in the list.

$$
\begin{array}{r}
7,200 \\
6,100 \\
6,000 \\
6,550 \\
7,350 \\
6,800 \\
7,500 \\
+ \ 6,300 \\
\hline
53,800
\end{array}
$$

2. Then divide the sum (53,800) by the number of addends (8).

$$
\begin{array}{r}
6,725 \\
8\,)\overline{53,800} \\
-48 \\
\hline
58 \\
-56 \\
\hline
20 \\
-16 \\
\hline
40 \\
-40 \\
\hline
0
\end{array}
$$

3. $53,800 \div 8 = 6,725$

The average surface temperature of these eight blue-white stars is 6,725°F.

Using a
Tape Measure or Ruler

Tape measures, metersticks, and rulers are tools for measuring length. Scientists use units such as kilometers, meters, centimeters, and millimeters when making length measurements.

Use a Meterstick

1. Work with a partner to find the height of your reach. Stand facing a chalkboard. Reach up as high as you can with one hand.

2. Have your partner use chalk to mark the chalkboard at the highest point of your reach.

3. Use a meterstick to measure your reach to the nearest centimeter. Measure from the floor to the chalk mark. Record the height of your reach.

Use a Tape Measure

1. Use a tape measure to find the circumference of, or distance around, your partner's head. Wrap the tape around your partner's head.

2. Find the line where the tape begins to wrap over itself.

3. Record the distance around your partner's head to the nearest millimeter.

Measuring Volume

A graduated cylinder, a measuring cup, and a beaker are used to measure volume. Volume is the amount of space something takes up. Most of the containers that scientists use to measure volume have a scale marked in milliliters (mL).

Measure the Volume of a Liquid

1. Measure the volume of some juice. Pour the juice into a measuring container.

2. Move your head so that your eyes are level with the top of the juice. Read the scale line that is closest to the surface of the juice. If the surface of the juice is curved up on the sides, look at the lowest point of the curve.

3. Read the measurement on the scale. You can estimate the value between two lines on the scale to obtain a more accurate measurement.

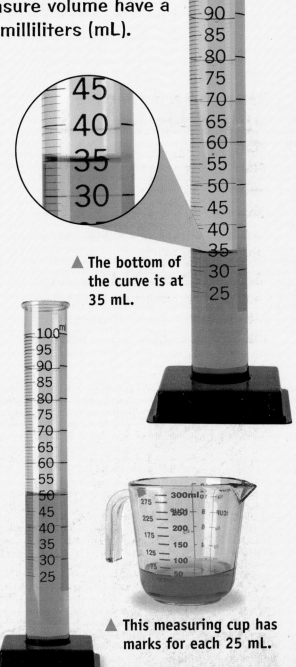

▲ The bottom of the curve is at 35 mL.

This beaker has marks for each 25 mL. ▶

This graduated cylinder has marks for every 1 mL. ▶

▲ **This measuring cup has marks for each 25 mL.**

Using a Thermometer

A thermometer is used to measure temperature. When the liquid in the tube of a thermometer gets warmer, it expands and moves farther up the tube. Different scales can be used to measure temperature, but scientists usually use the Celsius scale.

Measure the Temperature of a Cold Liquid

1. Half fill a cup with chilled liquid.

2. Hold the thermometer so that the bulb is in the center of the liquid. Be sure that there are no bright lights or direct sunlight shining on the bulb.

3. Wait until you see the liquid in the tube of the thermometer stop moving. Read the scale line that is closest to the top of the liquid in the tube. The thermometer shown reads 21°C (about 70°F).

Using a
Balance

A balance is used to measure mass. Mass is the amount of matter in an object. To find the mass of an object, place the object in the left pan of the balance. Place standard masses in the right pan.

Measure the Mass of a Ball

1. Check that the empty pans are balanced, or level with each other. The pointer at the base should be on the middle mark. If it needs to be adjusted, move the slider on the back of the balance a little to the left or right.

2. Place a ball on the left pan. Notice that the pointer moves and that the pans are no longer level with each other. Then add standard masses, one at a time, to the right pan. When the pointer is at the middle mark again, the pans are balanced. Each pan is holding the same amount of matter, and the same mass.

3. Each standard mass is marked to show its number of grams. Add the number of grams marked on the masses in the pan. The total is the mass of the ball in grams.

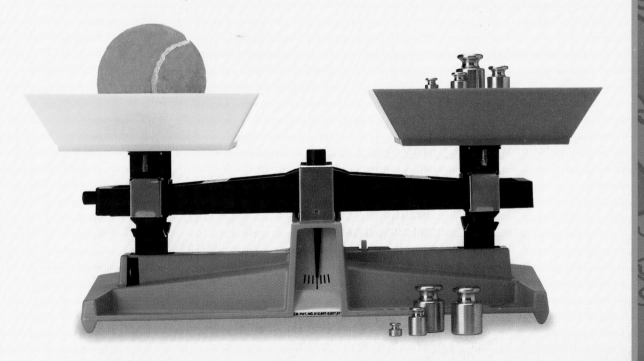

Using an
Equation or Formula

Equations and formulas can help you to determine measurements that are not easily made.

Use the Diameter of a Circle to Find Its Circumference

Find the circumference of a circle that has a diameter of 10 cm. To determine the circumference of a circle, use the formula below.

$$C = \pi d$$

$$C = 3.14 \times 10$$

$$C = 31.4 \text{ cm}$$

π is the symbol for pi. Always use 3.14 as the value for π, unless another value for pi is given.

The circumference of this circle is 31.4 cm.

The circumference (C) is a measure of the distance around a circle.

The diameter (d) of a circle is a line segment that passes through the center of the circle and connects two points on the circle.

Use Rate and Time to Determine Distance

Suppose an aircraft travels at 772 km/h for 2.5 hours. How many kilometers does the aircraft travel during that time? To determine distance traveled, use the distance formula below.

$$d = rt$$

$$d = 772 \times 2.5$$

$$d = 1,930 \text{ km}$$

d = distance

r = rate, or the speed at which the aircraft is traveling.

t = the length of time traveled

The aircraft travels 1,930 km in 2.5 hours.

Making a Chart to Organize Data

A chart can help you record, compare, or classify information.

Organize Properties of Elements

Suppose you collected the data shown at the right. The data presents properties of silver, gold, lead, and iron.

You could organize this information in a chart by classifying the physical properties of each element.

My Data

Silver (Ag) has a density of 10.5 g/cm³. It melts at 961°C and boils at 2,212°C. It is used in dentistry and to make jewelry and electronic conductors.

Gold melts at 1,064°C and boils at 2,966°C. Its chemical symbol is Au. It has a density of 19.3 g/cm³ and is used for jewelry, in coins, and in dentistry.

The melting point of lead (Pb) is 328°C. The boiling point is 1,740°C. It has a density of 11.3 g/cm³. Some uses for lead are in storage batteries, paints, and dyes.

Iron (Fe) has a density of 7.9 g/cm³. It will melt at 1,535°C and boil at 3,000°C. It is used for building materials, in manufacturing, and as a dietary supplement.

Create categories that describe the information you have found.

Give the chart a title that describes what is listed in it.

Properties of Some Elements

Element	Symbol	Density g/cm³	Melting Point (°C)	Boiling Point (°C)	Some Uses
Silver	Ag	10.5	961	2,212	jewelry, dentistry, electric conductors
Gold	Au	19.3	1,064	2,966	jewelry, dentistry, coins
Lead	Pb	11.3	328	1,740	storage batteries, paints, dyes
Iron	Fe	7.9	1,535	3,000	building materials, manufacturing, dietary supplement

Make sure the information is listed accurately in each column.

Reading a Circle Graph

A circle graph shows the whole divided into parts.
You can use a circle graph to compare parts to each
other or to compare parts to the whole.

Read a Circle Graph of Land Area

The whole circle represents the approximate land area of all
of the continents on Earth. The number on each wedge
indicates the land area of each continent. From the graph
you can determine that altogether the land area of the
continents is 148,000,000 square kilometers.

Together
Antarctica and
Australia are
about equal to
the land area of
North America.

Africa accounts
for more of the
Earth's land area
than South
America.

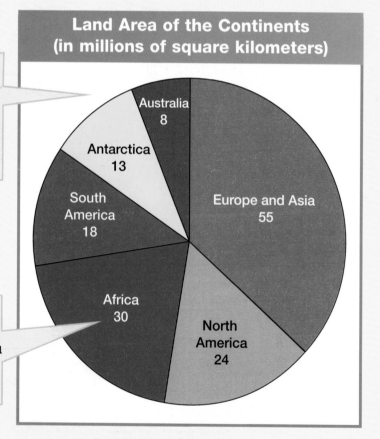

**Land Area of the Continents
(in millions of square kilometers)**

Australia
8

Antarctica
13

South
America
18

Europe and Asia
55

Africa
30

North
America
24

Making a Line Graph

A line graph is a way to show continuous change over time. You can use the information from a table to make a line graph.

Make a Line Graph of Temperatures

The table shows temperature readings over a 12-hour period at the Dallas–Fort Worth Airport in Texas. This data can also be displayed in a line graph that shows temperature change over time.

Dallas–Fort Worth Airport Temperature	
Hour	Temp. (°C)
6 A.M.	22
7 A.M.	24
8 A.M.	25
9 A.M.	26
10 A.M.	27
11 A.M.	29
12 NOON	31
1 P.M.	32
2 P.M.	33
3 P.M.	34
4 P.M.	35
5 P.M.	35
6 P.M.	34

1. Choose a title. The title should help a reader understand what your graph describes.

2. Choose a scale and mark equal intervals. The vertical scale should include the least value and the greatest value in the set of data.

3. Label the horizontal axis *Time* and the vertical axis *Temperature (°C)*.

4. Write the hours on the horizontal axis. Space the hours equally.

5. Carefully graph the data. Depending on the interval you choose, some temperatures will be between two numbers.

6. Check each step of your work.

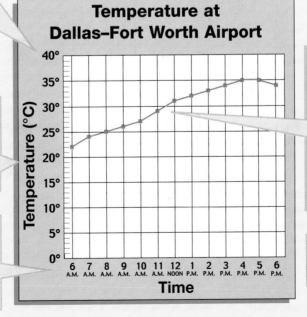

Temperature at Dallas–Fort Worth Airport

Finding
Range, Median, and Mode

You probably know that an average is a way to describe a set of data. Other ways to describe a set of data include range, median, and mode. The data in the table show the speeds at which various animals can run.

Speeds of Animals	
Animal	**Speed (km/h)**
White-tailed deer	48
Hyena	64
Cheetah	113
Squirrel	19
Zebra	64
Rabbit	56
Human	45

Finding the Range

The **range** can tell you if the data is spread far apart or clustered. To find the range, subtract the least number from the greatest number in a set of data.

$$113 - 19 = 94$$

The difference, or range, of the data is 94.

| 19 | 45 | 48 | 56 | 64 | 64 | 113 |

Finding the Median

The **median** is the middle number or the average of the two middle numbers when the data is arranged in order. The middle or median of the data set is 56.

Finding the Mode

The **mode** is the number or numbers that occur most often in a set of data. Sometimes there is no mode or more than one mode. The number that occurs most often is 64.

Using a
Spring Scale

A spring scale is used to measure force.
You can use a spring scale to find the weight
of an object in newtons. You can also use
the scale to measure other forces.

Measure the Weight of an Object

1. Place the object in a net bag and hang it from
the hook on the bottom of the spring scale. Or, if
possible, hang the object directly from the hook.

2. Slowly lift the scale by the handle at the top.
Be sure the object to be weighed continues to hang
from the hook.

3. Wait until the indicator inside the clear tube
of the spring scale has stopped moving. Read the
number next to the indicator. This number is the
weight of the object in newtons.

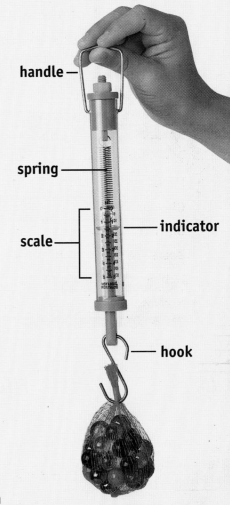

handle —

spring —

scale —

— indicator

— hook

Measure Friction

1. Hang the object from the hook at the bottom of
the spring scale. Use a piece of string to connect the
hook and object if needed.

2. Gently pull the handle at the top of the scale
parallel to the floor. When the object starts to move,
read the number of newtons next to the indicator on
the scale. This number is the force of friction between
the floor and the object as you drag the object.

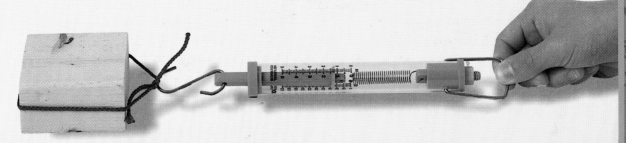

MEASUREMENTS

Volume
1 L of sports drink is a little more than 1 qt.

Area
A basketball court covers about 4,700 ft². It covers about 435 m².

Mass and Weight
A basketball has a mass of about 650 g. It weighs about $1\frac{1}{2}$ lb.

Metric Measures

Temperature
Ice melts at 0 degrees Celsius (°C)

Water freezes at 0°C

Water boils at 100°C

Length and Distance
1,000 meters (m) = 1 kilometer (km)

100 centimeters (cm) = 1 m

10 millimeters (mm) = 1 cm

Force
1 newton (N) =
  1 kilogram x meter/second/second
  (kg x m/s²)

Volume
1 cubic meter (m³) = 1 m x 1 m x 1 m

1 cubic centimeter (cm³) =
  1 cm x 1 cm x 1 cm

1 liter (L) = 1,000 milliliters (mL)

1 cm³ = 1 mL

Area
1 square kilometer (km²) = 1 km x 1 km

1 hectare = 10,000 m²

Mass
1,000 grams (g) = 1 kilogram (kg)

1,000 milligrams (mg) = 1 g

Temperature

The temperature at an indoor basketball game might be 25°C, which is 77°F.

Length/Distance

A basketball rim is about 10 ft high, or a little more than 3 m from the floor.

Customary Measures

Temperature

Ice melts at 32 degrees Fahrenheit (°F)

Water freezes at 32°F

Water boils at 212°F

Length and Distance

12 inches (in.) = 1 foot (ft)

3 ft = 1 yard (yd)

5,280 ft = 1 mile (mi)

Weight

16 ounces (oz) = 1 pound (lb)

2,000 pounds = 1 ton (T)

Volume of Fluids

8 fluid ounces (fl oz) = 1 cup (c)

2 c = 1 pint (pt)

2 pt = 1 quart (qt)

4 qt = 1 gallon (gal)

Metric and Customary Rates

km/h = kilometers per hour

m/s = meters per second

mph = miles per hour

GLOSSARY

Pronunciation Key

Symbol	Key Words	Symbol	Key Words
a	cat	g	get
ā	ape	h	help
ä	cot, car	j	jump
		k	kiss, call
e	ten, berry	l	leg
ē	me	m	meat
		n	nose
i	fit, here	p	put
ī	ice, fire	r	red
		s	see
ō	go	t	top
ô	fall, for	v	vat
oi	oil	w	wish
͞o	look, pull	y	yard
o͞o	tool, rule	z	zebra
ou	out, crowd		
		ch	chin, arch
u	up	ŋ	ring, drink
ʉ	fur, shirt	sh	she, push
		th	thin, truth
ə	a in ago	*th*	then, father
	e in agent	zh	measure
	i in pencil		
	o in atom		
	u in circus		
b	bed		
d	dog		
f	fall		

A heavy stress mark (′) is placed after a syllable that gets a heavy, or primary, stress, as in **picture** (pik′chər).

A

abyssal plain (ə bis′əl plān) The broad, flat ocean bottom. (E34) The *abyssal plain* covers nearly half of Earth's surface.

acceleration (ak sel ər ā′shən) The rate at which velocity changes over time. (F21) The spacecraft's *acceleration* increased as it soared into the air.

acid (as′id) A compound that turns blue litmus paper to red and forms a salt when it reacts with a base. (C81) *Acids* have a sour taste.

action force The initial force exerted in a force-pair. (F90) When you push against something, you are applying an *action force*.

active transport The process by which the cell uses energy to move materials through the cell membrane. (A17) Food molecules are moved into a cell by *active transport*.

aftershock A less powerful shock following the principal shock of an earthquake. (B56) Many *aftershocks* shook the ground in the days after the major earthquake.

algae (al′jē) Any of various mostly single-celled plantlike protists. (A34) Diatoms and seaweed are kinds of *algae*.

alloy (al′oi) A solution of two or more metals. (C59) Bronze is an *alloy* of copper and tin.

antibiotic (an tī bī ät′ik) A substance, often produced by microbes or fungi, that can stop the growth and reproduction of bacteria. (A57) Doctors prescribe *antibiotics* to treat various diseases.

antibody (an′ti bäd ē) A protein produced in the blood that destroys or weakens bacteria and viruses. (A57) *Antibodies* are produced in response to infection.

aquaculture (ak′wə kul chər) The raising of water plants and animals for human use or consumption. (E78) Raising catfish on a catfish "farm" is a form of *aquaculture*.

archaeologist (är kē äl′ə jist) A scientist who studies ancient cultures by digging up evidence of human life from the past. (B90) *Archaeologists* discovered human remains in the ancient city of Pompeii.

asexual reproduction (ā sek′shoo al rē prə duk′ shən) Reproduction involving a cell or cells from one parent that results in offspring exactly like the parent. (D10) The division of an amoeba into two cells is an example of *asexual reproduction*.

asthenosphere (as then′ə sfir) The layer of Earth below the lithosphere; the upper part of the mantle. (B36) The *asthenosphere* contains hot, partially melted rock with plasticlike properties.

astronomical unit A unit of measurement equal to the distance from Earth to the Sun. (F9) Pluto is 39.3 *astronomical units* (A.U.) from the Sun.

atom The smallest particle of an element that has the chemical properties of that element. (C35) An *atom* of sodium differs from an *atom* of chlorine.

atomic number (ə täm'ik num'bər) The number of protons in the nucleus of an atom. (C73) The *atomic number* of oxygen is 8.

bacteria (bak tir'ē ə) Monerans that feed on dead organic matter or on living things. (A49) Diseases such as pneumonia and tuberculosis are caused by *bacteria*.

base A compound that turns red litmus paper blue and that forms a salt when it reacts with an acid. (C81) *Bases* have a slippery feel.

benthos (ben'thäs) All the plants and animals that live on the ocean bottom. (E25) The *benthos* group include oysters, crabs, and coral.

blue-green bacteria (bloo grēn bak tir'ē ə) Monerans that contain chlorophyll. (A49) Like plants, *blue-green bacteria* carry out photosynthesis and make their own food.

budding A form of asexual reproduction in which a new individual develops from a bump, or bud, on the body of the parent. (D13) Some one-celled organisms, such as yeast, reproduce by *budding*.

buoyancy (boi'ən sē) The upward force exerted by a fluid on objects submerged in the fluid. (F121) Objects float better in salt water than in fresh water because salt water has greater *buoyancy*.

caldera (kal der'ə) A large circular depression, or basin, at the top of a volcano. (B102) The eruption formed a *caldera* that later became a lake.

cast fossil (kast fäs'əl) A fossil formed when minerals from rock move into and harden inside the space left by a decaying organism. (D55) *Cast fossils* of shells can provide information about the animals from which the fossils formed.

cell The basic unit that makes up all living things. (A9) The human body is made up of trillions of *cells*.

cell differentiation (sel dif ər en-shē ā'shən) The development of cells into different and specialized cell types. (A25) Through *cell differentiation*, plant cells and animal cells develop into tissues.

cell membrane (sel mem'brān) The structure that surrounds and encloses a cell and controls the movement of substances into and out of the cell. (A10) The *cell membrane* shrank when the cell was placed in salt water.

cell respiration (sel res pə rā'shən) The process in cells in which oxygen is used to release stored energy by breaking down sugar molecules. (A19) The process of *cell respiration* provides energy for a cell's activities.

cell theory A theory that explains the structure of all living things. (A10) The *cell theory* states that all living things are made up of cells.

cell wall The rigid structure surrounding the cells of plants, monerans, and some protists. (A10) The *cell wall* gives a cell its rigid shape.

chemical change A change in matter that results in one or more new substances with new properties. (C69) A *chemical change* occurs when wood burns and forms gases and ash.

chemical formula A group of symbols and numbers that shows the elements that make up a compound. (C40) The *chemical formula* for carbon dioxide is CO_2.

chemical properties Characteristics of matter that describe how it changes when it reacts with other matter. (C34) The ability to burn is a *chemical property* of paper.

chemical symbol One or two letters used to stand for the name of an element. (C36) Ca is the *chemical symbol* for calcium.

20
Ca
Calcium

chloroplast (klôr'ə plast) A tiny green organelle that contains chlorophyll and is found in plant cells and some protist cells. (A10) The chlorophyll inside a *chloroplast* enables a plant cell to capture solar energy.

chromosome (krō'mə sōm) A threadlike structure in the nucleus of a cell; it carries the genes that determine the traits an offspring inherits from its parent or parents. (A10, D22) Most cells in the human body contain 23 pairs of *chromosomes*.

cinder cone A kind of volcano, usually steep-sloped, that is formed from layers of cinders, which are sticky bits of volcanic material. (B86) *Cinder cones* result from explosive eruptions.

communicable disease (kə myo͞o'ni-kə bəl di zēz) A disease that can be passed from one individual to another. (A58) Bacteria, which are easily passed from organism to organism, are the cause of many *communicable diseases*.

competition (käm pə tish'ən) The struggle among organisms for available resources. (D77) *Competition* among members of a species is a factor in evolution.

composite cone (kəm päz′it kōn) A kind of volcano formed when explosive eruptions of sticky lava alternate with quieter eruptions of volcanic rock bits. (B89) Mount Vesuvius is a *composite cone* in southern Italy.

compound (käm′pound) A substance made up of two or more elements that are chemically combined. (C34) Water is a *compound* made up of hydrogen and oxygen.

condensation (kän dən sā′shən) The change of state from a gas to a liquid. (C28) The *condensation* of water vapor can form droplets of water on the outside of a cold glass.

continental edge (kän tə nent″l ej) The point at which the continental shelf, which surrounds each continent, begins to angle sharply downward. (E33) Beyond the *continental edge* the ocean increases rapidly in depth.

continental rise The lower portion of the continental slope, extending to the deep ocean floor. (E33) The *continental rise* slopes downward to the deepest part of the ocean.

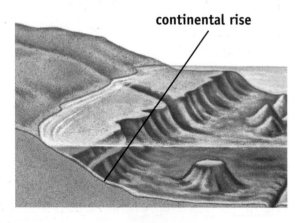
continental rise

continental shelf The gently sloping shelf of land extending from the shoreline to the continental edge. (E32) The *continental shelf* can extend hundreds of miles out into the ocean.

continental slope The steep clifflike drop from the continental edge to the deep ocean floor. (E33) The *continental slope* connects the continental shelf with the ocean bottom.

controlled experiment A test of a hypothesis in which the setups are identical in all ways except one. (S7) In the *controlled experiment*, one beaker of water contained salt.

convection (kən vek′shən) The process by which heat energy is transferred through liquids or gases. (B37) The air was heated by *convection*.

convection current The path along which energy is transferred during convection. (B37) Scientists think that *convection currents* in the mantle cause Earth's tectonic plates to move.

convergent boundary (kən vur′jənt boun′də rē) A place where the plates that make up Earth's crust and upper mantle collide or come together. (B38) Layers of rock may bend or break at a *convergent boundary*.

Coriolis effect (kôr ē ō′lis e fekt′) The tendency of a body or fluid moving across Earth's surface to have a curving motion due to Earth's rotation. (E54) The *Coriolis effect* causes air and water currents to move clockwise in the Northern Hemisphere.

crest The top of a wave. (E63) The *crest* of the wave seemed to tower over the surfer.

crust The thin outer layer of Earth. (B19) Earth's *crust* varies in thickness from 5 km to 48 km.

current Great rivers of water moving through the ocean. (E53) The strong *current* pulled the boat away from shore.

cytoplasm (sīt'ō plaz əm) The watery gel inside a cell. (A11) Various organelles, including vacuoles and mitochondria, are found inside the *cytoplasm* of a cell.

deceleration (dē sel ər ā'shən) A decrease in speed over time. (F23) Air resistance can cause the *deceleration* of objects.

density The amount of mass in a given volume of matter. (C13) Lead has a greater *density* than aluminum.

desalination (dē sal ə nā'shən) A process for obtaining fresh water from salt water by removing the salt. (E78) A few countries operate *desalination* plants, which obtain fresh water from ocean water.

diatom (dī'ə täm) A microscopic, one-celled algae with a glasslike cell wall. (A34) A single liter of sea water may contain millions of *diatoms* of various kinds.

diffusion (di fyoo'zhən) The movement of substances from an area of greater concentration to an area of lesser concentration. (A16) Oxygen can pass in and out of cells by *diffusion*.

divergent boundary (dī vʉr'jənt boun'də rē) A place where the plates that make up Earth's crust and upper mantle move away from one another. (B38) Most *divergent boundaries* are found on the floor of the ocean.

dome mountain A mountain formed when magma lifts Earth's surface, creating a broad dome, or bulge. (B45) Pikes Peak in Colorado is a *dome mountain.*

domesticated (dō mes'ti kāt əd) Tamed or bred to serve people's purposes. (D68) People breed *domesticated* animals such as horses for transportation and other uses.

dominant trait (däm'ə nənt trāt) A trait that will be expressed if it is inherited. (D43) Gregor Mendel found that tallness was a *dominant trait* in pea plants.

drag A force that resists forward motion through a fluid; it operates in the direction opposite to thrust. (F109) The air causes *drag* on an airplane.

earthquake A shaking or movement of Earth's surface, caused by the release of stored energy along a fault. (B56) Many *earthquakes* occur near the boundaries between tectonic plates.

electron (ē lek′trän) A negatively charged particle in an atom. (C71) The number of *electrons* in an atom usually equals the number of protons.

element (el′ə mənt) A substance that cannot be broken down into any other substance by ordinary chemical means. (C34) Oxygen, hydrogen, copper, iron, and carbon are *elements*.

endangered species A species of animal or plant whose number has become so small that the species is in danger of becoming extinct. (D25) The black-footed ferret is an *endangered species* that is found in North America.

epicenter (ep′i sent ər) The point on Earth's surface directly above an earthquake's point of origin, or focus. (B63) The *epicenter* of the earthquake was 2 km north of the city.

era (ir′a) One of the major divisions of geologic time. (D57) Many kinds of mammals developed during the Cenozoic *Era*.

ethanol (eth′ə nôl) A kind of alcohol used to make medicines, food products, and various other items. (A40) *Ethanol* is a flammable liquid that can be used as a fuel.

evaporation (ē vap ə rā′shən) The change of state from a liquid to a gas. (C27) Heat from the Sun caused the *evaporation* of the water.

evolution (ev ə lōō′shən) The development of new species from earlier species over time. (D56) According to the theory of *evolution*, the plants and animals alive today descended from organisms that lived millions of years ago.

extinct (ek stiŋkt′) No longer in existence; having no living descendant. (D25) Dinosaurs and mammoths are both *extinct*.

extinction (ek stiŋk′shən) The disappearance of species from Earth. (D60) Scientists do not agree about what caused the *extinction* of the dinosaurs.

fault A break in rock along which rock slabs have moved. (B63) The shifting of Earth's tectonic plates can produce a *fault*, along which earthquakes may occur.

fault-block mountain A mountain formed when masses of rock move up or down along a fault. (B45) Mountains in the Great Rift Valley of Africa are *fault-block mountains.*

fermentation (fŭr mən tā′shən) A chemical change in which an organism breaks down sugar to produce carbon dioxide and alcohol or lactic acid. (A19) The action of yeast caused *fermentation* in the sugary liquid.

fertilization (fŭr tə li zā′shən) The process by which a sperm and an egg unite to form a cell that will develop into a new individual. (D24) In humans, *fertilization* produces a cell containing 46 chromosomes, half from the female parent and half from the male parent.

fetch (fech) The distance the wind blows over open water. (E64) The longer the *fetch*, the bigger the waves become.

first law of motion The concept that objects at rest tend to remain at rest and objects in motion tend to remain in motion, traveling at a constant speed and in the same direction. (F59) According to the *first law of motion*, a stationary object will stay in place unless some force causes the object to move.

fission (fish′ən) A method of asexual reproduction in which a parent cell divides to form two identical new cells. (A32, D10) Many one-celled organisms, such as amoebas, reproduce by *fission.*

focus (fō′kəs) The point, or place, at which an earthquake begins. (B63) The *focus* of the earthquake was about 20 km beneath Earth's surface.

folded mountain A mountain formed when two tectonic plates collide. (B43) The Alps and the Himalayas are *folded mountains.*

force A push or a pull. (F33) The *force* of friction caused the rolling wagon to slow and then stop.

fossil (fäs′əl) The remains or traces of a living thing, usually preserved in rock. (D54) *Fossils* are usually found in sedimentary rock.

freezing The change of state from a liquid to a solid. (C28) The *freezing* of water occurs at 0°C.

friction (frik′shən) A force that resists motion between two surfaces that are in contact with each other. (F73) *Friction* keeps a car's tires from slipping off the road.

fungi (fun′jī) Organisms that feed on dead organisms or that are parasitic. (A41) Most *fungi* attach to and grow on organic matter.

G

gene (jēn) One of the units that make up a chromosome; genes determine the traits an offspring inherits from its parent or parents. (D33) Half of your *genes* come from your mother, and half come from your father.

gene splicing (jēn spli'siŋ) A process by which genes are manipulated to alter the function or nature of an organism, usually by being transferred from one organism to another. (D45) Through *gene splicing*, scientists have transferred a gene for making insulin from one organism to another.

genetic engineering (jə net'ik en-jə nir'iŋ) The process by which genes are manipulated to bring about biological change in species. (D46) Using *genetic engineering* techniques, scientists have successfully combined DNA from different organisms.

gravity (grav'i tē) The force that pulls objects toward Earth; also, the attractive force exerted by a body or an object on other bodies or objects. (F33) *Gravity* causes a ball to fall to the ground after it is thrown into the air.

heat Energy that flows from warmer to cooler regions of matter. (C26) *Heat* can cause matter to change from one state to another.

hot spot A place deep within Earth's mantle that is extremely hot and contains a chamber of magma. (B100) Magma rising from a *hot spot* can break through Earth's crust to form a volcano.

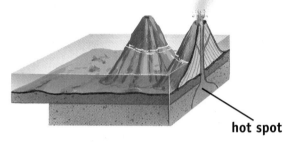

hot spot

hypothesis (hī päth'ə sis) An idea about or explanation of how or why something happens. (S6) The *hypothesis* about the expanding universe has been supported by evidence gathered by astronomers.

I

immune system (im myo͞on' sis'təm) The body system that defends the body against diseases. (A56) The *immune system* produces antibodies to fight disease.

incomplete dominance (in kəm-plēt' däm'ə nəns) The expression of both genes (traits) in a pair, producing a blended effect. (D44) A plant with pink flowers, produced by crossing a plant having red flowers with a plant having white flowers, is an example of *incomplete dominance*.

indicator (in'di kāt ər) A substance that changes color when mixed with an acid or a base. (C81) Paper treated with an *indicator* is used to test whether a compound is an acid or a base.

inertia (in ur′shə) The tendency of an object to remain at rest if at rest, or if in motion, to remain in motion in the same direction. (F59) *Inertia* results in passengers in a car moving forward when the driver applies the brakes.

inherited trait (in her′it əd trāt) A trait that is passed on from parents to offspring through genes. (D32) Eye color is an *inherited trait*.

ion (ī′ən) An electrically charged atom. (C73) *Ions* form when atoms lose or gain electrons. Sodium chloride is made up of sodium *ions* and chlorine *ions*.

island arc A chain of volcanoes formed from magma that rises as a result of an oceanic plate sinking into the mantle. (B94) The Philippine Islands are part of an *island arc*.

kinetic energy (ki net′ik en′ər jē) Energy of motion. (C25) A ball rolling down a hill has *kinetic energy*.

___L___

lava (lä′və) Magma that flows out onto Earth's surface from a volcano. (B85) Flaming *lava* poured down the sides of the volcanic mountain.

law of conservation of momentum The principle that states that momentum can be transferred but cannot be lost. (F84) The *law of conservation of momentum* explains why the momentum resulting from the collision of two objects equals the total momentum of the objects before they collided.

learned trait A trait that is not passed on in DNA, but instead is acquired through learning or experience. (D34) The ability to speak Spanish is a *learned trait*.

lift The upward force, resulting from differences in air pressure above and below an airplane's wings, that causes the airplane to rise. (F109) Increasing the size of an airplane's wings increases *lift*.

lithosphere (lith′ō sfir) The solid, rocky layer of Earth, including the crust and top part of the mantle. (B36) The *lithosphere* is about 100 km in thickness.

magma (mag′mə) The hot, molten rock deep inside Earth. (B84) The *magma* rose from the underground chamber through the volcano.

magnetic field The space around a magnet within which the force of the magnet is exerted. (B26) The magnet attracted all the iron filings within its *magnetic field*.

magnetic reversal (mag net'ik ri-vʉr'səl) The switching or changing of Earth's magnetic poles such that the north magnetic pole becomes located at the south magnetic pole's position and vice versa. (B26) Scientists have found evidence of *magnetic reversals* in layers of rock along the ocean floor.

magnitude (mag'nə to͞od) The force or strength of an earthquake. (B57) *Magnitude* is a measure of the amount of energy released by an earthquake.

mantle The layer of Earth between the crust and the core. (B19) The *mantle* is made up of a thick layer of rock.

mass The amount of matter in an object. (C10, F32) A large rock has more *mass* than a pebble.

matter Anything that has mass and volume. (C10, F32) Rocks, water, and air are three kinds of *matter.*

meiosis (mī ō'sis) The process of cell division by which sex cells receive half the number of chromosomes as other body cells. (D22) Because of *meiosis*, a sex cell in a human has only 23 chromosomes instead of 46.

melt To change state from a solid to a liquid. (C27) The icicles began to *melt.*

metric system A system of measurement based on a few defined units and in which larger and smaller units are related by powers of 10. (F11) In the *metric system*, a centimeter is 10 times longer than a millimeter.

mid-ocean ridge A chain of mountains on the ocean floor. (B27, E34) New ocean floor forms at the *mid-ocean ridge.*

mitochondria (mīt ō kän'drē ə) Cell organelles in which energy is released from food. (A11) The more *mitochondria* a cell has, the more energy it can release from food.

mitosis (mī tō'sis) The process in which one cell divides to form two identical new cells. (A23) The new cells that are formed by *mitosis* have the same number of chromosomes as the parent cell.

mixture A combination of two or more substances that can be separated by physical means. (C34) This jar contains a *mixture* of colored beads.

model Something used or made to represent an object or to describe how a process takes place. (C71) The plastic *model* showed the structure of the heart.

mold fossil (mōld fäs'əl) A fossil consisting of a hollowed space in the shape of an organism or one of its parts. (D54) Footprints of animals left in mud that dried in the sun became a type of *mold fossil.*

molecule (mäl'i kyo͞ol) A particle made up of a group of atoms that are chemically bonded. (C39) A *molecule* of water contains two hydrogen atoms and one oxygen atom.

momentum (mō men'təm) A property of a moving object, calculated by multiplying the object's mass by its velocity. (F82) The train gathered *momentum* as its speed increased.

moneran (ma nir'ən) Any one-celled organism in which the cell does not have a nucleus. (A48) Bacteria are *monerans.*

multicellular (mul ti sel'yo͞o lər) Made up of more than one cell. (A32) Some protists are *multicellular.*

mutation (myo͞o tā'shən) A change in a gene's DNA that can result in a new characteristic, or trait. (D74) Certain *mutations* have helped species survive in their environment.

natural selection (nach'ər əl sə-lek'shən) The process by which those living things that have characteristics that allow them to adapt to their environment tend to live longest and produce the most offspring, passing on these favorable characteristics to their offspring. (D73) *Natural selection* helps explain why certain characteristics become common while others die out.

neap tide (nēp tīd) The tide occurring at the first and third quarters of the Moon, when the difference in level between high and low tide is smallest. (E69) *Neap tides* occur twice each month.

nekton (nek'tän) All the free-swimming animals that live in the ocean. (E25) The *nekton* group includes such active animals as fish, octopuses, and whales.

neutralization (no͞o trə lī zā'shən) The reaction between an acid and a base. (C83) *Neutralization* produces water and a salt.

neutron (no͞o'trän) A particle in the nucleus of an atom that has no electric charge. (C71) The mass of a *neutron* is about equal to the mass of a proton.

newton (no͞o'tən) A unit used to measure force in the metric system. (F67) A *newton* is the force needed to accelerate a one-kilogram object by one meter per second every second.

nuclear fission (no͞o'klē ər fish'ən) The splitting of the nucleus of an atom, releasing great amounts of energy. (C77) Bombarding a nucleus with neutrons can cause *nuclear fission.*

nuclear membrane The structure that surrounds the nucleus and controls what substances move into and out of the nucleus. (A11) The *nuclear membrane* appears to be solid, but it actually has tiny holes through which materials can pass.

nucleus (noo'klē əs) 1. The control center of a cell. (A11) The *nucleus* contains the cell's genetic information. 2. The dense, central part of an atom. (C71) The *nucleus* is made up of protons and neutrons and contains nearly all of an atom's mass.

organ A part of a multicellular organism made up of a group of tissues that work together to perform a certain function. (A25) The heart, stomach, brain, and the lungs are *organs* of the human body.

organ system A group of organs that work together to perform one or more functions. (A26) The bones are part of the *organ system* that supports the body.

osmosis (äs mō'sis) The diffusion of water through a membrane. (A16) Water enters and leaves a cell through the process of *osmosis*.

paleontologist (pā lē ən täl'ə jist) A scientist who studies fossils. (D56) A team of *paleontologists* discovered the remains of a dinosaur.

Pangaea (pan jē'ə) A supercontinent that existed about 200 million years ago. (B9) *Pangaea* broke apart into several continents.

period 1. A division of geologic time that is a subdivision of an era. (D57) The Jurassic *Period* is part of the Mesozoic Era. 2. The time it takes for two successive waves to pass the same point. (E63) The *period* for the ocean waves was about ten seconds.

petrification (pe tri fi kā'shən) The changing of the hard parts of a dead organism to stone. (D55) Fossils of trees have been preserved by *petrification*.

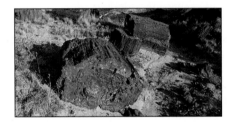

photosynthesis (fōt ō sin'thə sis) The process by which green plants and other producers use light energy to make food. (A18, E24) In *photosynthesis*, plant cells use light energy to make sugar from carbon dioxide and water.

physical change A change in size, shape, or state of matter, with no new kind of matter being formed. (C68) The freezing of water into ice cubes is an example of a *physical change*.

physical properties Characteristics of matter that can be measured or detected by the senses. (C34) Color is a *physical property* of minerals.

phytoplankton (fīt ō plaŋk'tən) The group of usually microscopic plant-like protists that live near the surface of the ocean. (E10) *Phytoplankton* drifts with the ocean currents.

plankton (plaŋk′tən) The group of organisms, generally microscopic in size, that float or drift near the ocean surface. (A34, E10) *Plankton* is a source of food for fish.

plate boundary A place where the plates that make up Earth's crust and upper mantle either move together or apart or else move past one another. (B20) Earthquakes occur along *plate boundaries.*

pollution The contamination of the environment with waste materials or other unwanted substances. (E89) Dangerous chemicals dumped into the ocean are one source of *pollution.*

polymer (päl′ə mər) An organic compound consisting of large molecules formed from many smaller, linked molecules. (C90) Proteins are *polymers.*

protist (prōt′ist) Any of a large group of mostly single-celled, microscopic organisms that have traits of plants, animals, or both. (A32) Parameciums and algae are *protists.*

proton (prō′tän) A positively charged particle found in the nucleus of an atom. (C71) The atomic number of an atom equals the number of *protons* in the atom's nucleus.

protozoan (prō tō zō′ən) A protist that has animal-like traits. (A32) A paramecium is a *protozoan.*

radioactive element (rā dē ō ak′tiv el′ə mənt) An element made up of atoms whose nuclei break down, or decay, into nuclei of other atoms. (C76) As the nucleus of a *radioactive element* decays, energy and particles are released.

reaction force The force exerted in response to an action force. (F90) A *reaction force* is equal in strength to an action force but opposite in direction to the action force.

recessive trait (ri ses′iv trāt) A trait that will not be expressed if paired with a dominant trait. (D43) In his experiments with pea plants, Gregor Mendel learned that shortness was a *recessive trait.*

reproduction (rē prə duk′ shən) The process by which organisms produce more of their own kind. (D10) *Reproduction* ensures the survival of the species.

Richter scale (rik′tər skāl) A scale of numbers by which the magnitude of earthquakes is measured. (B56) Each increase of 1.0 on the *Richter scale* represents an increase of about 30 times the energy released by an earthquake.

rifting (rift′iŋ) The process by which magma rises to fill the gap between two plates that are moving apart. (B106) *Rifting* in eastern Africa may split the continent into two parts.

salinity (sə lin'ə tē) The total amount of dissolved salts in ocean water. (E9) The *salinity* of the ocean varies in different parts of the world.

salt A compound that can be formed when an acid reacts with a base. (C83) When vinegar and baking soda interact, they produce a *salt* and water.

saprophyte (sap'rə fīt) An organism that lives on dead or decaying matter. (A42) Molds are *saprophytes*.

sea-floor spreading The process by which new ocean floor is continually being formed as magma rises to the surface and hardens into rock. (B28) *Sea-floor spreading* occurs as magma fills the space between separating plates.

seamount (sē'mount) An underwater mountain that formed from a volcano. (E34) Thousands of *seamounts* rise from the floor of the Pacific.

second law of motion The concept that an object that is at rest or in motion will not change its condition unless something causes the change. (F65) A gust of wind blowing an open umbrella out of your hands illustrates the *second law of motion*.

seismograph (sīz'mə graf) An instrument that records the intensity, duration, and nature of earthquake waves. (B72) Scientists use information from *seismographs* to determine the location of earthquakes.

seismometer (sīz mäm'ə tər) An instrument that detects and records Earth's movements. (B96) Data from the *seismometer* suggested that a volcanic eruption might soon occur.

selective breeding Breeding of living things to produce offspring with certain desired characteristics. (D68) People have used *selective breeding* to produce domesticated animals.

sex cell A female or male reproductive cell; an egg cell or sperm cell. (D22) Reproduction can occur when *sex cells* unite.

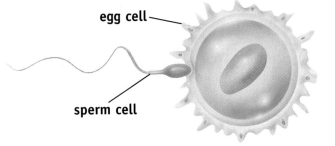

egg cell

sperm cell

sexual reproduction Reproduction that involves the joining of a male sex cell and a female sex cell. (D22) Most animals and plants produce offspring through *sexual reproduction*.

shield cone A kind of volcanic cone that is large and gently sloped and that is formed when lava flows quietly from a crack in the Earth's crust. (B87) Mauna Loa, a *shield cone* in Hawaii, is the largest volcano on Earth.

solute (säl'yо̄о̄t) The material present in the smaller amount in a solution; the substance dissolved in a solution. (C57) If you dissolve sugar in water, sugar is the *solute*.

solution A mixture in which the different particles are spread evenly throughout the mixture. (C57) Dissolving salt in water makes a *solution.*

solvent (säl′vənt) The material present in the greater amount in a solution; the substance in a solution, usually a liquid, that dissolves another substance. (C57) If you mix sugar and water, water is the *solvent.*

speed The distance traveled in a certain amount of time; rate of movement. (F16) The truck was moving at a *speed* of 40 mph.

spore A reproductive cell that can develop into a new organism. (A41) Ferns and mushrooms produce *spores.*

spring tide An extremely high tide or low tide occurring at or just after the new moon and full moon. (E69) At the time of a *spring tide*, both the Sun and the Moon are in line with Earth.

state of matter Any of the three forms that matter may take: solid, liquid, or gas. (C20) Water's *state of matter* depends on its temperature.

substance (sub′stəns) Matter that always has the same makeup and properties, wherever it may be found. (C34) Elements and compounds are *substances.*

tectonic plate (tek tän′ik plāt) One of the slabs that make up Earth's crust and upper mantle; also called *tectonic plate.* (B19) Some of Earth's *tectonic plates* carry continents.

temperature A measure of the average kinetic energy of the particles in matter. (C26) Water *temperature* rises as the motion of water molecules increases.

theory (thē′ ə re) A hypothesis that is supported by a lot of evidence and is widely accepted by scientists. (S9) The Big Bang *Theory* offers an explanation for the origin of the universe.

theory of continental drift A theory that states that the continents formed a single landmass at one time in the past and have drifted over time to their present positions. (B10) The *theory of continental drift* was first suggested by Alfred Wegener.

theory of plate tectonics The theory that Earth's lithosphere is broken into enormous slabs, or plates, that are in motion. (B19) Scientists use the *theory of plate tectonics* to explain how Earth's continents drift.

third law of motion The concept that for every action force there is an equal and opposite reaction force. (F90) When you watch someone's feet bouncing off a trampoline, you see the *third law of motion* at work.

thrust (thrust) The push or driving force that causes an airplane, rocket, or other object to move forward. (F108) *Thrust* can be produced by a spinning propeller or by a jet engine.

tide The daily rise and fall of the level of the ocean or other large body of water, caused by the gravitational attraction of the Moon and the Sun. (E68) As the *tide* came in, we moved our blanket back from the water's edge.

tiltmeter (tilt'mēt ər) An instrument that measures any change in the slope of an area. (B96) Scientists use *tiltmeters* to note any bulges that form in a mountain's slopes.

tissue A group of similar, specialized cells working together to carry out the same function. (A25) Muscle *tissue* contains cells that contract.

toxin (täks'in) A chemical poison that is harmful to the body. (A54) *Toxins* produced by bacteria can cause serious illness.

trade wind A planetary wind that blows from east to west toward the equator. (E54) South of the equator, the *trade wind* comes from the southeast.

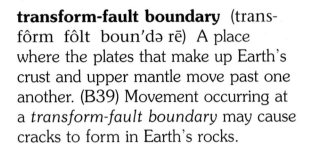

transform-fault boundary (transfôrm fôlt boun'də rē) A place where the plates that make up Earth's crust and upper mantle move past one another. (B39) Movement occurring at a *transform-fault boundary* may cause cracks to form in Earth's rocks.

tsunami (tso͞o nä'mē) A huge, powerful ocean wave usually caused by an underwater earthquake. (B74) A *tsunami* can cause great destruction.

turbidity current (tʉr bid'i tē kʉr'ənt) A current of water carrying large amounts of sediment. (E59) *Turbidity currents* may cause sediment to build up in some places.

upwelling The rising of deep water to the surface that occurs when winds move surface water. (E58) *Upwelling* brings pieces of shells and dead organisms up from the ocean floor.

vaccine (vak sēn') A preparation of dead or weakened bacteria or viruses that produces immunity to a disease. (A57) The *vaccine* for smallpox has eliminated that disease.

vacuole (vak'yo͞o ōl) A structure in the cytoplasm in which food and other substances are stored. (A11) A *vacuole* in a plant cell is often quite large.

variable (ver'ē ə bəl) The one difference in the setups of a controlled experiment; provides a comparison for testing a hypothesis. (S7) The *variable* in an experiment with plants was the amount of water given to each plant.

vegetative propagation (vej ə tāt'iv präp ə gā'shən) A form of asexual reproduction in which a new plant develops from a part of a parent plant. (D14) Using a cutting taken from a houseplant to grow a new plant is a method of *vegetative propagation.*

velocity (və läs'ə tē) The rate of motion in a particular direction. (F21) The *velocity* was northwest at 880 km/h.

virus (vī'rəs) A tiny disease-causing agent consisting of genetic material wrapped inside a capsule of protein. (A50) *Viruses* cause such diseases as AIDS, chickenpox, and rabies.

volcano An opening in Earth's crust through which hot gases, rock fragments, and molten rock erupt. (B86) Lava flowed out of the *volcano.*

volume (väl'yo͞om) The amount of space that matter takes up. (C11) A large fuel tank holds a greater *volume* of gasoline than a small tank.

wave The up-and-down movement of the surface of water, caused by the wind. (E63) Ocean *waves* crashed against the shoreline.

wavelength The distance between two successive waves. (E63) At the height of the storm, the waves had a *wavelength* of 10 m.

weight A measure of the force of gravity on an object. (F33) The *weight* of this package is five pounds.

westerly (wes'tər lē) A prevailing wind that blows from west to east. (E54) Ships that sailed from North America to Europe were aided by the power of the *westerlies.*

zooplankton (zō ō plaŋk'tən) The group of tiny animal-like organisms that live near the surface of the ocean. (E11) *Zooplankton* float in the sea.

zygote (zī'gōt) A fertilized egg cell. (D24) A *zygote* develops into an embryo by means of cell division.

INDEX

* Activity

* **Activity**

CREDITS

ILLUSTRATORS

Cover: Mike Quon.

Think Like a Scientist: 14: Laurie Hamilton. *Border:* Mike Quon.

Unit A 10–11: Teri McDermott. 13: Eldon Doty. 17: Michael Kress-Russick. 18–19: Ray Vella. *t.* Carlyn Iverson. 22–23: Keith Kasnot. 25: Walter Stuart. 26: *t.* Michael Kress-Russick; *m.* Briar Lee Mitchell; *b.* Michael Kress-Russick. 32: Virge Kask. 33: Kirk Moldoff. 37: Yvonne Walston. 41–42: David Flaherty. 48, 51: Barbara Cousins. 52–53: Eldon Doty. 59–60: Ken Tiessen. 61, 63: Barbara Cousins.

Unit B 7: Dolores Bego. 8–9: Eldon Doty. 10: Dale Glasgow & Assoc. 11: Claudia Karabaic Sargent. 12–15: Ray Smith. *maps:* Geo Systems. 17, 18: Eureka Cartography. 19: Warren Budd. 20: *l.* Warren Budd. 20–21: Eureka Cartography. 24–25: Greg Harris. 26: Bill Morris. 27: Greg Harris. 28: Delores Bego. 29: Warren Budd. 31: Eureka Cartography. 36, 37: Brad Gaber. 38: *m.r.* Brad Gaber. 38, 39: Julie Carpenter. 41: Eureka Cartography. 43, 45, 46: Bob Swanson. 47: *t.* Randy Verougstraete; *b.* Ben Perini. 49, 53: Eureka Cartography. 54–55: Eldon Doty. 57: Eureka Cartography. 58: Robert Schuster. 62: *t.* Bob Brugger. *b.* Robert Roper. 63, 65: Robert Roper. 73: Joe Spencer. 74–75: *border:* Julie Carpenter; *b.* Greg Harris; *t.r.* Dolores Bego. 76: Julie Carpenter. 77, 78: Patrick Gnan. 79: Robert Roper. 84: Bob Swanson. 85: Dolores Bego. 86, 87: John Youssi. 88: Eureka Cartography. 90: Laszlo Kubini. 91: Eldon Doty. 94: *t.* Laszlo Kubini. 94–95: Bob Swanson. 99: Eureka Cartography. 100: *t.l.* Eureka Cartography; *r.* Greg Harris. 100–101: Greg Harris. 103: Dale Glasgow & Assoc. 105: Stephen Bauer. 106–107: John Youssi. 107: *t.* Robert Roper. 108: *l.* Eureka Cartography; *r.* Susan Johnson Carlson. 109: Greg Harris. 111: Eldon Doty.

Unit C 3: Olivia McElroy. 10–11: Andrew Shiff. 12: *t.* Andrew Shiff; *b.* Scott Ross. 15: Terry Boles. 19–21: Scott Ross. 26–27: Robert Pasternack. 29: Patrick Gnan. 34: Bill Fox. 36–37: Paul Woods. 39–41: Nadine Sokol. 51: Bob Brugger. 56: Patrick Gnan. 57: Bob Radigan. 58: Adam Mathews. 61: Paul Woods. 69: Patrick Gnan. 70, 72–74: Nadine Sokol. 75: Eldon Doty. 76: *m.l.* George Hardebeck; *b.r.* Ken Rosenborg. 77: Ken Rosenborg. 82–83: Steven Mach. 88: Patrick Gnan. 90, 92: Robert Schuster.

Unit D 3: Olivia McElroy. 10–12: Karl Edwards. 14, 16–17: Wendy Smith-Griswold. 19, 21, 23: J.A.K. Graphics. 24: Kirk Moldoff. 32–34: Terri McDermott. 35: *border:* Terri McDermott, Terry Kovalcik. 36, 38: Barbara Cousins. 40: Linda Nye. 42–44: Marjorie Muns. 46: Terri McDermott. 54–55: David Uhl. 57: *b.l.* Andy Lendway; *t.r.* Raymond Smith. 58–59: Raymond Smith. 60: Richard Courtney. 64–65: Christine Schaar. 66–67: Drew Brook Cormack. 68: Rosemary Volpe. 72–74: Mona Conner. 75: Tina Fong. 77: Andy Lendway. 79: Patrick Gnan.

Unit E 8–11: Bob Radigan. 11: *t.* Robert Shuster. 17: *t.m.* Terry Boles. 24, 25: Jim Salvati. 32–33: Joe McDermott. 36–39: *t.* Steven Nau. 36: Jon Prud'Homme. 38: Stephan Wagner. 39: Jeff Seaver. 41: Barbara Hoopes Ambler. 42–43: Bob Radigan. 43: Eldon Doty. 47: Joe McDermott. 53, 54: Peter Spacek. 54: Jeffrey Hitch. 56–57: Adam Mathews. 57: *b.* Jeffrey Hitch. 58–59: Adam Mathews. 60–61: Steven Nau. 63: *t.* Catherine Leary. *b.* Greg Harris. 68, 69: Jon Prud'Homme. 71: Greg Harris. 78: Michael Sloan. 80–81: Eldon Doty. 82–83, 84: Gary Torrisi. 89: Dean St. Clair. 90–91: *b.* Bob Radigan; *t.* Dean St. Clair.

Unit F 3: Olivia McElroy. 8–10: Terry Boles. 14: A.J. Miller. 16–17: Jeffery Oh. 24: Art Cummings. 25: Linda Richards. 26: David Klug. 27: Terry Boles. 32–33, 35: Terry Boles. 38: Eldon Doty. 43: Rebecca Merriles. 46: Lois Leonard Stock. 47: Don Dixon. 48–49: Larry Jost. 55–57: Michael Sloan. 58–59: Scott Ross. 60–61: Jeffery Lynch. 65: Terry Boles. 73–79: Linda Richards. 82: Sergio Roffo. 91: Bob Novak. 93, 101: Larry Jost. 104–105: Terry Boles. 108–109: Patrick Gnan. 115: Terry Boles. 121–122: Peter Spacek. 123: *border:* Peter Spacek; *b.* Bob Novak. 124: Peter Spacek. 125, 127: Patrick Gnan.

Science and Math Toolbox: *Logos:* Nancy Tobin. 14–15: Andrew Shiff. *Borders:* Mike Quon.

Glossary 20: Terri McDermott. 21: *b.l.* Paul Woods;p *m.r.* John Youssi. 22: Joe McDermott. 23: John Youssi. 26: Greg Harris. 27: Nadine Sokol. 28: Patrick Gnan. 29: Barbara Cousins. 31: Terri McDermott. 32: Kirk Moldoff. 33: John Prud'Homme. 34: Jeffery Hitch. 35: Barbara Cousins.

PHOTOGRAPHS
All photographs by Houghton Mifflin Company (HMCo.) unless otherwise noted.

Front Cover: *t.* Robert Brons/BPS/Tony Stone Images; *m.l.* A. Witte/C. Mahaney/Tony Stone Images; *m.r.* Superstock; *b.l.* © Ken Eward/Bio Grafix-Science Source/Photo Researchers, Inc.; *b.r.* Alan Schein/The Stock Market.

Table of Contents: iii: *l.* © Don Fawcett/Photo Researchers, Inc.; *r.* © Biophoto Associates/Science Source/Photo Researchers, Inc. xi: Ken Lax for HMCo.

Think Like a Scientist: 3: *m.b.* Zig Leszczynski/Animals Animals/Earth Scenes; *b.* Fred Habegger/Grant Heilman Photography, Inc.

Runk/Schoenberger/Grant Heilman Photography, Inc.; *b.r.* Jim Strawser/Grant Heilman Photography, Inc. 17: *t.* Larry Lefever/Grant Heilman Photography, Inc.; *b.* Grant Heilman Photography, Inc. 22: © David M. Phillips/Photo Researchers, Inc. 25: The Granger Collection. 26: *t.* Ron Garrison/The Zoological Society of San Diego; *b.* Steve Kaufman/DRK Photo. 27: © M. Abbey/Photo Researchers, Inc. 28–29: *bkgd.* Dr. Jack Hearn/U.S. Department of Agricultural Research; *inset* Dr. Jack Hearn/U.S. Department of Agricultural Research. 31–33: Grant Huntington for HMCo. 34: *l.* Focus On Sports; *m.* Michael Ponzini/Focus On Sports; *r.* Sports Chrome. 37: Grant Huntington for HMCo. 39: Grant Huntington for HMCo. 42: Bill Horseman Photography/Stock Boston. 43: Austrian Cultural Institute. 44: Courtesy, Marcu Rhoades. 45: *l.* David M. Dennis/Tom Stack & Associates; *r.* David M. Dennis/Tom Stack & Associates. 48–49: *bkgd.* © Sinclair Stammers/Science Photo Library/Photo Researchers, Inc.; *inset* Courtesy, Jorge O. Calvo. 49: Courtesy, Jorge O. Calvo. 50: Ken Lax for HMCo. 51: *t.* Ken Lax for HMCo.; *m.* Breck Kent/Animals Animals/Earth Scenes; *m.* Kevin Aitken/Peter Arnold, Inc.; *b.r.* Breck Kent/Animals Animals/Earth Scenes. 52–53: Ken Lax for HMCo. 55: *l.* Wendell Metzen/Bruce Coleman; *r.* John Cancalosi/Peter Arnold, Inc. 56: *l.* Hinterleitner/Liaison International; *m.t.* Kenneth Garrett/© National Geographic Society; *m.b.* Kenneth Garrett/© National Geographic Society; *r.* Kenneth Garrett/© National Geographic Society. 61: *bkgd.* NASA; *inset* Peter Ward. 66: © Darwin Museum. 69: *l.* Sean Sprague/Impact Visuals; *r.* Larry Lefever/Grant Heilman Photography, Inc. 71: Ken Lax for HMCo. 75: E.R. Degginger/Color-Pic, Inc. 76: J.&C. Kroeger/Animals Animals/Earth Scenes.

Unit E 1–3: © 1997 Telegraph Colour Library/FPG International. 4–5: *bkgd.* Dave Fleetham/Pacific Stock; *inset* New Jersey News Photos. 8: *l.* © Francois Gohier/Photo Researchers, Inc.; *r.* William Johnson/Stock Boston. 9: *t.* William Johnson/Stock Boston; *b.* © Carl Purcell/Photo Researchers, Inc. 10: *t.* © Gregory Ochoki/Photo Researchers, Inc.; *b.* Ralph Oberlander/Stock Boston. 17: Michael Grecco/Stock Boston. 18–19: Thomas J. Abercrombie/© National Geographic Society. 20: *t.* Norbert Wu; *b.* Jack Stein Grove/PhotoEdit. 24: *t.* © Eric Grave/Science Source/Photo Researchers, Inc.; *b.* © D.P. Wilson/Science Source/Photo Researchers, Inc. 25: *t.* © Charles V. Angelo/Photo Researchers, Inc.; *b.* Larry Tackett/Tom Stack & Associates. 26: *l.* Frank Oberlander/Stock Boston; *r.* Dave Fleetham/Pacific Stock. 27: *l.* © Charles V. Angelo/Photo Researchers, Inc.; *r.* Frank Oberlander/Stock Boston. 28–29: *bkgd.* Greg Vauhgn/Tom Stack & Associates; *inset* Courtesy, Scientific Search Project. 34: Jim Watt/Pacific Stock. 35: *t.* Jeff Greenberg/The Picture Cube. 37: *t.* Superstock ; *b.l.* Peter Parks/Mo Yung Productions/Norbert Wu Wildlife Photographer; *b.r.* NOAA Photo Library, U.S. Dept. of Commerce. 43: *t.* Woods Hole Oceanographic Institution; *m.* Stephanie Compoint/Sygma Photo News; *b.* The Bettmann Archive. 44: *t.* Michael Holford; *b.* Michael Holford. 45: *t.* Michael Holford; *b.* Michael Holford. 46: Wildlife Conservation Society. 48–49: *bkgd.* AP/Wide World Photos; *inset* Ann Summa for HMCo. 53: NASA. 55: *l.* © 2000 Adam Woolfitt/Woodfin Camp and Associates; *r.* © 2000 Momatiuk/Eastcott/Woodfin Camp and Associates. 56: Superstock. 57: John Beatty/Oxford Scientific/Animals Animals/Earth Scenes. 58: *t.* © Francois Gohier/Photo Researchers, Inc.; *b.* E.R. Degginger/Color-Pic, Inc. 59: George Goodwin/Color-Pic, Inc. 60–61: Ken Karp for HMCo. 64: *t.* Erik Aeder/Pacific Stock. 65: The Bettmann Archive. 69: The Bettmann Archive. 70: *l.* © Groenendyk/Photo Researchers, Inc.; *r.* Bill Bachmann/Stock Boston. 72–73: *bkgd.* Jack Stein Grove/PhotoEdit; *inset* Courtesy, Natural Energy Laboratory of Hawaii Authority. 73: Courtesy, Natural Energy Laboratory of Hawaii Authority. 75: Ken Karp for HMCo. 77: border Richard Hutchings for HMCo.; *b.l.* Larry Brock/Tom Stack & Associates; *b.r.* Thomas D. Magelsen/Peter Arnold, Inc. 78: *l.* Greg Vaughn/Tom Stack & Associates; *r.* © Porterfield-Chickering/Photo Researchers, Inc. 79: *t.r.* Runk/Schoenberger/Grant Heilman Photography, Inc.; *b.l.* Runk/Schoenberger/Grant Heilman Photography, Inc. 81: *t.* J&L Weber/Peter Arnold, Inc.; *b.* © Andrew J. Martinez/Photo Researchers, Inc. 82: Greg Ryan & Sally Beyer/Positive Reflections. 85: *l.* Nancy Dudley/Stock Boston; *r.* Nancy Dudley/Stock Boston. 86–88: Ken Karp for HMCo. 89: *t.* Stacy Pick/Stock Boston; *b.* Steve Austin/Papilio/Corbis. 91: *t.* NASA; *b.* Robert Winslow/Tom Stack & Associates. 92: Exxon Co., U.S.A. 93: John Paul/FSP/Liaison International.

Unit F 1: Operation Migration Inc. 2–3: Operation Migration Inc. 4–5: *bkgd.* James L. Amos/Corbis; *inset* Kevin Jackson. 11: Imagery/Picture Perfect USA Inc. 15: Courtesy, Edwards Air Force Base. 21: Courtesy, Wet 'N Wild. 22: © NASA/Mark Marten/Science Source/Photo Researchers, Inc. 23: Co Rentmeester/The Image Bank. 28–29: *bkgd.* John Turner/Tony Stone Images; *l.* Carolyn Russo/National Air and Space Museum Smithsonian Institution; *r.* Budd Davison/Courtesy, Smithsonian Institution. 39: *l.* Al Tielemans/Duomo Photography; *r.* David Madison Photography. 40–41: Courtesy, Estes Industries. 45: E. Bordis/Leo de Wys. 46: NASA. 48: Tom Sanders/The Stock Market. 50: Corbis. 52–53: Express Newspapers/Archive Photos. 58: Superstock. 59: Jeff Foott/Bruce Coleman. 61: Romilly Lockyer/The Image Bank. 63: *b.* © H. Zwarc/Petit Format/Photo Researchers, Inc. 66: Leverett Bradley/Tony Stone Images. 66–67: Globus Brothers for HMCo. 69: Steven Pumphey/© National Geographic Society. 73: Richard T. Bryant/Aristock, Inc. 75: Reuters/Gary Cameron/Archive Photos. 78–79: *bkgd.* Nina Bermann/Sipa Press; *inset* Engineered Demolition. 82: Henry Groskinsky/Peter Arnold, Inc. 83: *t.* © Jerry Wachter/Photo Researchers, Inc.; *b.* Mitchell Layton/Duomo Photography. 84: Rick Rickman/Duomo Photography. 85: NASA/Corbis. 87: Globus Studios, Inc. 88: Grant Huntington for HMCo. 89: Focus On Sports. 96: Erich Lessing/Art Resource, NY. 97: *t.* Kingston Collection/Profiles West; *b.* © George Holton/Photo Researchers, Inc. 98: *t.* Kim Taylor/Bruce Coleman; *b.* Bruce Coleman. 99: David Madison Photography. 100: Stephen Frink/Southern Stock Photo Agency. 102–103: NASA. 107: North Wind Picture Archives. 111: Bruno de Hogues/Tony Stone Images. 116: *l.* Corbis; *m.* The Granger Collection; *r.* NASA. 117: Roger Ressmeyer/Corbis. 121: Paul Kenward/Tony Stone Images. 122: Richard Megna/Fundamental Photographs. 124: Adam Zetter/Leo de Wys.

Science and Math Toolbox 2: *r.* Grant Huntington for HMCo.

Glossary 24: Steve Kaufman/DRK Photo. 25: © Sidney Moulds/Photo Researchers, Inc. 30: Wendell Metzen/Bruce Coleman.